Exploring Faith and ' orld
Emily R. Brink and P

Wise Church

FAITH
ALIVE.

Grand Rapids, Michigan

We gratefully acknowledge permission from the World Communion of Reformed Churches to include the document "Worshiping the Triune God," and we also thank the Calvin Institute of Christian Worship for its encouragement and support.

Unless otherwise noted, Scripture quotations in this publication are from The Holy Bible, New International Version® NIV®. Copyright © 1973, 1978, 1984, 2011 by Biblica, Inc.™ Used by permission. All rights reserved world-wide.

Cover art: *Angels of the Four Directions* by Laura James. Used by permission.

Photos from the Calvin Institute of Christian Worship stock unless indicated. Used by permission.

Wise Church: Exploring Faith and Worship with Christians around the World, © 2013, Faith Alive Christian Resources, 2850 Kalamazoo Ave. SE, Grand Rapids, MI, 49560.

Printed in the United States of America.

We welcome your comments. Call us at 1-800-333-8300 or email us at editors@faithaliveresources.org.

ISBN: 978-1-59255-786-8

10 9 8 7 6 5 4 3 2 1

Contents

Introduction

A song from Canada

Come, now is the time to worship;
come, now is the time to give your heart.
Come just as you are to worship;
come just as you are before your God.
Come.

One day every tongue will confess you are God.
One day every knee will bow,
still the greatest treasure remains for those
who gladly choose you now.

Come, now is the time to worship;
come, now is the time to give your heart.
Come just as you are to worship;
come just as you are before your God.
Come.

From: "Come, Now Is The Time to Worship"
Words: Brian Doerksen © 1998 Vineyard Songs, admin. in North America by Music Services, Inc.

Welcome to this study! In these five sessions we'll take a look at what millions of people do each week as they gather for worship in many different places and in many different ways.

The way your congregation worships is both similar to and different from the way other Christian communities worship, whether they're across the street or across the world. So how can we speak of Christian worship in a way that gets at the root of what it means to worship God in community? In this study we will take a closer look at our own practices, viewed through "the bigger picture" that transcends any local setting.

Development of "Worshiping the Triune God"

Our basic text will be the document "Worshiping the Triune God" (WTG), a set of wisdom proverbs distilled from Scripture and gathered from people around the world. It was developed in preparation for the inaugural meeting of the World Communion of Reformed Churches in 2010. The leaders preparing for that meeting requested a document that could help root this new communion in a theology of worship. They observed, "The word *communion* in our new name needs to be rooted in worship, which is at the heart of our life together as Christians." Their goal was that in all our diversity we may seek the unity of the body of Christ in our worship.

An international committee was appointed, early drafts were sent far and wide, and during the meetings of the World Communion of Reformed Churches held at Calvin College in June 2010, the final editing took place. "Worshiping the Triune God" has been translated into Chinese, Dutch, German, French, Indonesian, and Spanish, and is in the process of being translated into other languages as well. The entire document is included in this book beginning on page 9; it is also available in different languages at www.wcrc.ch or www.worship.calvin.edu.

Rather than producing an essay on the theology of worship, the committee turned to proverbs—a literary form rooted in wisdom literature and embedded in many cultures for millennia. Even today, proverbs help people around the world, especially those in oral cultures, pass down wisdom from one generation to the next (Google "Bangladesh proverbs," for example). As we will see in the proverbs in this document, the framework for worship is blessing. We gather, not first of all to be blessed, but because God has *already* blessed us. In our worship together, more blessings await us (WTG 1.3).

A Word about This Study

Emily Brink was a member of the international committee that developed "Worshiping the Triune God," and Paul Detterman wrote a number of articles in *Reformed Worship* (Reformed Worship.org) introducing its wisdom. Together they have now written this study—a conversation in dialogue with "Worshiping the Triune God." Their hope is that churches far and near may develop a culture of learning about the central activity of the

Christian church: our worship of the God who has called us, loves us, blesses us, and to whom we offer our adoration and praise.

How we understand God and God's plans for us has a significant impact on what we anticipate and how we participate in worship. As this conversation progresses, we will have the opportunity to touch mystery, not only the great mystery of the Trinity but also the mystery of God's relationship with us and with all of creation. These proverbs about the worship of God, like Jesus' parables about the kingdom of God, help us find the trailhead as we begin to explore in greater depth the wonder, awe, beauty, and joy that awaits us.

Our goals for this study are:

- to gain a greater understanding of why we worship as we do.

- to increase our joy and deepen our fellowship with the triune God, who invites us to worship and meets us there.

- to acknowledge and celebrate unity in the body of Christ at the font and around the table, in our need for confession and experience of grace, and in our mutual language of praise, prayer, and faith profession.

- to affirm that we are called by God to worship in order that we can be sent by God to be and to make disciples of Jesus Christ.

Structuring the Sessions

This study has five main sections, each one focusing on a different section of "Worshiping the Triune God." Those five sections reflect the shape of Christian worship of every time and place, regardless of style or setting: Gathering, Proclamation, Response, Celebrating, and Sending.

Each main section is divided into "A" and "B" subsections. The five "A" subsections examine the five sections of "Worshiping the Triune God." The five "B" subsections are entitled "Going Deeper," and offer additional opportunity for conversation and reflection.

We hope that worship committees, worship teams, pastors, elders, and adult education groups will find a place to approach the conversation. There are many possible ways to structure the study sessions. For example:

- Schedule a five-week study, covering both the A and B subsections in one session.

- Schedule a ten-week study, addressing each A and B subsection in a separate session.

- Schedule two five-week studies, studying sessions 1-A through 5-A in the first study and sessions 1-B through 5-B in the second study.

- Use selected sections for mini-discussions on a particular aspect of worship (e.g., a focus on baptism or on the proclamation of God's Word).

- Use this study as a ten-month in-depth discussion for church leaders such as elders, deacons, and worship planners.

In whatever way you use this study, our hope is that it will open your eyes to the majesty, mystery, and wonder of worshiping the triune God, and that it will deepen your own discipleship so that others will more clearly see Christ living in you.

> All praise and thanks to God the Father now be given,
> the Son and Spirit blest, who reign in highest heaven—
> the one eternal God, whom earth and heaven adore;
> for thus it was, is now, and shall be evermore.

From: "Now Thank We All Our God"
Words: Martin Rinkart, 1636; tr. Catherine Winkworth, 1863, alt., P.D.

Worshiping the Triune God:
Receiving and Sharing Christian Wisdom across Continents and Centuries

Adopted in 2010 by the World Communion of Reformed Churches

I. A Called and Forgiven People: Assembling in Jesus' Name

1.1 Called by the Triune God

Blessed are the people of God
who are deeply aware
that they are both called by and address the triune God,
Father, Son, and Holy Spirit,
who gathers, protects, and cares for the church
through Word and Spirit—[1]
a God of splendour and majesty
perfectly revealed in Jesus Christ,
the "image of the invisible God" (Col. 1:15).

Blessed is the community
that gratefully acknowledges
that the triune God not only receives our worship,
but also makes our worship possible,
prompting us through the Holy Spirit,
and sanctifying our offerings
through the perfect priesthood of Jesus Christ,
who during his life on earth offered
praise "to the Father," "full of joy in the Holy Spirit"
(Luke 10:21),
and even now "ever lives to pray for us" (Heb. 7:25).

Blessed is the congregation
that insists that believers gather to worship God
not, first of all, in order that God might bless them,
but because God has already blessed them.

Blessed is the congregation that then discovers
that God does indeed bless them
as they worship the triune God
who nourishes, teaches, convicts, and corrects them,
and strengthens bonds
that unite believers with Jesus Christ and with each other
through the sanctifying actions
of the proclamation of the Word and corporate prayer,
through baptism and the Lord's Supper,
through fellowship, offerings, and testimony.

[1] Heidelberg Catechism Q&A 54; Belhar Confession 1

1.2 Corporate Assembly, the Whole People of God

Wise is the worshiping community
that "does not neglect meeting together" (Heb. 10:25),
but joyfully gathers in Jesus' name,
eager to proclaim the Word of God,
to offer praise and prayer,
and to celebrate the sacraments,
each of which are actions of the whole people of God,
"the royal priesthood" (1 Pet. 2:9).

Blessed is the congregation
that invites all worshipers—
including those which our cultures
may label in different ways as "disabled"—
to full, conscious, and active participation in corporate worship,
engaging heart, soul, and mind in devotion to God,
deeply aware of how their own personal worship
participates in a much larger chorus of praise to God.

Blessed is the congregation
that expresses in its worship
the communion in the body of Christ,
the unity of the Spirit in the bond of peace,
and the oneness that is the gift and calling of God
that unites the young and old
and believers of every time and place
who share a common calling by the Spirit of God in Jesus
Christ.[2]

[2] from WCRC materials for the inaugural assembly in Grand Rapids, Michigan.

1.3 The Holy Spirit

Wise is the worshiping community
that recognizes how the Holy Spirit works
through both reason and emotion,
through both spiritual disciplines and surprising events,
through both services that are prayerfully planned
and through moments of spontaneous discovery.

Wise is the worshiping community that recognizes that
the lasting value or spiritual power of worship
does not depend upon our own creativity,
imagination, intellect, or emotions,
but comes from the Holy Spirit,
who may choose to use any or all of these things.
For, truly, worship is a gift to receive,
not an accomplishment to achieve.

1.4 Affirming and Resisting Culture

Wise is the church
that seeks to be "in" but not "of" the world (John 15:19),
resisting aspects of the culture
that compromise the integrity of the gospel,
and eagerly engaging its culture
with the good news of the gospel of Jesus Christ
who comes to each culture but is not bound by any culture.

Wise, then, is the church
that is grateful that the gospel of Jesus
is at once transcultural, contextual,
cross-cultural, and countercultural.[3]

---

[3] Cf the Lutheran World Federation's Nairobi Statement on Worship and Culture

1.5 The Goodness of the Redeemed Creation

Wise is the congregation
that makes clear that its worship
participates in the song of praise
that is offered by all creation.

Wise is the congregation
that celebrates worship as an embodied reality,
grateful for the gestures and postures

that express our praise and prayer,
and the book, water, bread, and wine
that God ordains for our use—
the gifts of God for the people of God.

1.6 Leading God's People

Wise is the community that
calls, trains, affirms, and responds to
those gifted for leadership in all genders, ages, races, and abilities,
providing formative training and mentorship for them
in the theology and practices of worship.

Wise are leaders in worship
who equip all the members of the community
for full, conscious, and active participation,
taking care to express hospitality
to those who are not yet a part of Christ's body, the church.

1.7 Artistic Expression

Blessed is the congregation in which the Word is proclaimed
and prayers and praise are offered
not only through words,
but also through artistic expression:
through gifts God has given
to each local community
in music and dance,
in speech and silence,
in visual art and architecture.
Blessed are the artists
who offer and discipline their gifts
so God's people may
testify to the goodness of God,
offer thanks, and express repentance.

Wise are artists who are grateful
both for the limitations offered by the second commandment,
and also for the example of the biblical artists called by God
and equipped by God's people for service
according to God's commands (Ex. 35:30ff).

Wise is the church
that gratefully receives
the gifts of faithful songs and artworks
from other centuries and other cultures,
celebrating the catholicity of the church
and cultivating creativity
through new songs and works for worship.

II. Joyfully Proclaiming God's Word

2.1 Word and Spirit

Blessed is the congregation
in which the Word of God is proclaimed
with conviction and joy,
surrounded by expectant prayers
and profound gratitude
for the Holy Spirit's work
to illuminate the hearts and minds of God's people.

2.2 The Breadth of the Christ-Centered Word

Wise is the congregation
that nourishes believers
with readings and sermons that engage
the breadth and depth of God's Word,
Old Testament and New Testament,
always proclaiming the fullness of the gospel of Jesus Christ.

2.3 Calling Forth Rest and Witness, Justice and Peace

Blessed is the congregation
in which the proclamation of God's Word
comforts those who mourn
and confronts those who oppose God's reign.

Wise is the preacher
who invites hearers to receive God's lavish grace,
to repent from sin and evil,
to turn toward Christ,
to proclaim peace,
"to do justice, to love kindness and to walk humbly with
God" (Mic. 6:8).

2.4 Resisting Idolatry

Wise is the congregation
that proclaims the Word of God
in ways that actively expose and resist
both the idols that we are tempted to worship instead of God
and also the idols of our distorted understandings of God.

Blessed is the congregation
that challenges these distortions
by contemplating the person and work of Jesus Christ,
"the radiance of God's glory and the exact representation of
God's being" (Heb. 1:3).

2.5 Credo: The Response of Faith

Wise is the congregation
in which the proclamation of the gospel
is accepted as the Word of God,
which is at work in you who believe (1 Thess. 2:13),
leading to both confession and praise,
both repentance and a commitment to service,
both compassion and a passion for justice,
both personal and communal actions,
both new obedience and profound gratitude.

Blessed is the congregation
that invites believers to testify to the goodness of God
by expressing the faith of the church
that transcends and forms our individual experiences
and unites us with believers across cultures and centuries,
and by testifying to the work of God in the life of the local
community.

III. Responding to God in Prayer and Offerings

3.1 Praise and Gratitude

Blessed is the church that
offers praise and thanksgiving (cf Ps. 50:14, Heb. 13:15),
not only extolling the beauty and glory of God,
but also contemplating, reciting,
and celebrating all that God has done
throughout history.

Wise is the congregation
that draws upon and learns from
the Bible's own narratively-shaped prayers
of praise and thanksgiving (e.g. Ps. 136)
as it gives form to its own prayer.

3.2 Praying in Jesus' Name, through the Spirit

Blessed is the church that prays in Jesus' name,
acknowledging our union with our ascended and
ever-present Lord.

Blessed is the worshiping community
that prays in and through the Holy Spirit,
desiring the gifts of the Holy Spirit,
and acknowledging that as we pray
the Holy Spirit helps us in our weakness,
interceding for us according to the will of God (Rom. 8:26, 27)
and resisting the "cosmic powers of this present darkness"
(Eph. 6:12).

3.3 Full Range of Human Experience

Wise is the church that,
following the example of the psalms,
encourages honest and trusting prayers to God
that express the full range of human experience—
the "anatomy of the soul"—[4]
spoken, sung, or silent,
danced, dramatized, or visualized—
prayers of celebration and lament,
trust and desperation,
supplication and intercession,
thanksgiving and confession,
healing and hope.

Blessed is the church that prays not only for its own needs,
but also for the needs of the world that God so loves.

---

[4] The phrase "anatomy of the soul" is from John Calvin's commentary on the psalms.

3.4 Gifts and Offerings

Wise is the church that gratefully practices
the giving of gifts, time, and talent
as an act of dedication and worship.

Wise is the church that affirms
that all of life is lived in service to God and neighbor,
and that believers are called to be stewards of every gift
of God.

IV. Baptizing and Feasting

4.1 Jesus' Commands to Baptize and Celebrate the Lord's Supper

Blessed is the church
that faithfully obeys Jesus' commands
"to make disciples,
baptizing them
in the name of the Father, Son, and Holy Spirit
and teaching them to obey
everything [Jesus has] commanded" (Matt. 28:20)
and to "eat and drink in remembrance of me" (Luke 22:19-20),
receiving these signs
as occasions in which God
works to nourish and sustain,
comfort and challenge,
teach and transform us.

4.2 Baptism

Blessed is the congregation
that announces that their true identity
is found in Jesus Christ.

Blessed is the congregation
that proclaims how the waters of baptism
are a sign and seal
of God's promises
to wash us clean,
to adopt us into the body of Christ,
to send the Holy Spirit to renew, empower,

and resurrect us to new life in Christ.

Blessed is the congregation
that proclaims how the waters of baptism
are also a sign and seal of God's call to renounce sin and evil,
to embrace Christ and our new identity in him,
and to live a renewed and holy life.

Wise is the community
that celebrates baptism joyfully
and remembers that baptism
is a means of grace and encouragement
to live out our vows of covenant faithfulness.

4.3 Lord's Supper

Blessed is the church
that regularly celebrates the Lord's Supper
as a feast of thanksgiving, communion, and hope.

Blessed is the congregation
that not only gratefully remembers God's
creating and redeeming work in Jesus Christ,
knowing his presence in the breaking of the bread,
but also gratefully receives the gift of union
with Jesus Christ and Christ's body,
and looks forward to the feast of the coming kingdom.

Blessed is the congregation
that shares this meal
by "discerning the body of Christ" in its manifold oneness,
by expressing hospitality for one another
with grace and truth (1 Cor. 11:29-33),
and by reflecting God's hospitality for us
in ministries of hospitality in the world.

V. A Blessed and Commissioned People Serving in Jesus' Name

5.1 God's Sending

Blessed is the congregation
in which believers are
encouraged by God's gracious blessing
and challenged by God's gracious call
to proclaim the good news of Jesus
and to live as a healing presence in the world
in the name of Jesus.

5.2 Daily Worship

Wise is the community
that nourishes faith
by encouraging daily worship for all believers,
with emphasis on reading and meditating on God's Word,
seeking the guidance of the Holy Spirit,
offering prayers of praise and petition,
singing psalms, hymns, and spiritual songs,
listening for God in "sheer silence" (1 Kings 19:12),
and living every moment before the face of God.

5.3 Hospitality and Evangelization

Blessed are communities
in which hospitality is practiced
in both public worship and in personal lives,
where strangers and guests are welcomed and embraced,
where the poor and marginalized, diseased and forsaken
can find refuge under the shadow of God's wings.

Blessed are communities
in which all people are invited and challenged
to become disciples of Jesus,
receiving baptism and formation in the faith (cf Matt. 28:19).

5.4 Formation for Worship

Wise are congregations
that invite and challenge believers
of all ages and abilities
to "grow in the grace and knowledge
of our Lord and Savior Jesus Christ" (2 Pet. 3:18).

Blessed are congregations
that nurture the faithful interplay
of Scripture, doctrines, practices, and the fruit of the Spirit.

Wise are congregations that deepen worship
through reflection on and teaching about
the meaning of worship practices.

5.5 Worship, Compassion, and Justice

Blessed are congregations
whose public worship points to Jesus Christ
and to Jesus' message about the
kingdom of God.

Blessed are congregations
whose corporate worship and public witness
are consistent with each other
and faithful to God's Word,
whose worship and witness are
a testimony to the work of the Holy Spirit.

Blessed are congregations who seek to receive
the liberating work of the Holy Spirit,
who alone can break through hypocrisy
and through whom
justice and peace, worship and witness,
can truly embrace.

5.6 Maranatha: Worship and Christian Hope

Blessed are congregations
who are not content
to live only in the present moment,
but whose worship expresses
the groaning of all creation
for the fullness of God's reign
in Jesus Christ.

Blessed are congregations whose
life together is summed up
in the certain hope of the prayer
"Maranatha—come, Lord Jesus" (Rev. 22:20).

A Gathering of Spirits by Jan Richardson. United States.
Used by permission.

Session 1: Gathering

A song from the United States

God, you call us to this place,
where we know your love and grace.
Here your hospitality makes of us one family,
makes our rich diversity richer still in unity,
makes our many voices one,
joined in praise with Christ your Son.

Now assembled in Christ's name,
all your mercies to proclaim—
in the hearing of your word,
in our prayer through Christ the Lord,
in the ministries we share,
learning how to serve with care—
in the Spirit let us be one in faith and unity.

In the water we were born of the Spirit in the Son.
Now a priestly, royal race rich in every gift of grace—
called, forgiven, loved, and freed,
for the world we intercede:
gather into unity all the human family.

Even in its simplest forms, Christian worship is multidimensional. Throughout the history of the church, disciples of Jesus experience at least three realities whenever we gather for worship:

1. We bring our context with us: trauma (natural disaster, violence, oppression, political upheaval, unemployment, relocation, death) combines with triumph (births,

graduations, new jobs, new relationships) to make us who we are on any given day. Even the most "stable" worshiping community will be "different" each time it gathers because our world is constantly changing and so are we.

2. Consciously or not, we are "logging on" to the unending worship of the triune God across creation and throughout time. No matter how edgy or how stodgy our particular worship may seem, no matter how connected or how isolated any group of worshipers may feel, we are all part of the cosmic reality hymn writer Maltbie Babcock called "the music of the spheres."

3. By the gift of the Holy Spirit, we can participate in the communion of the triune God. This is possible because of the ongoing work of Jesus the Christ. James Torrance says, "There is only one offering which is truly acceptable to God, and it is not ours. It is the offering by which [Christ] has sanctified for all time those who come to God by him."

—Worship, Community & the Triune God of Grace, by James B. Torrance
InterVarsity Press, 1996, p. 21

Authentic Christian worship, like the Word of God on which it is centered, is living, breathing, changing, vibrant, vital, refreshingly unpredictable, and always transformative. The blessing of worship, the life-changing experience of encountering and praising the Father, Son, and Spirit, is available to disciples of Jesus every time we gather. This blessing is not dependent on our resources, the beauty of our location, the approval of our culture, or any other temporal circumstance. It is a gift from God.

Session 1-A

1.1 Called by God: Why Gather?

Blessed are the people of God who are deeply aware that they are both called by and address the triune God, Father, Son, and Holy Spirit, who gathers, protects, and cares for the church through Word and Spirit—a God of splendour and majesty perfectly revealed in Jesus Christ, the "image of the invisible God" (Col. 1:15).

Blessed is the community that gratefully acknowledges that the triune God not only receives our worship, but also makes our worship possible, prompting us through the Holy Spirit, and sanctifying our offerings through the perfect priesthood of Jesus Christ, who during his life on earth offered praise to the Father, "full of joy in the Holy Spirit" (Luke 10:21), and even now "ever lives to pray for us" (Heb. 7:25).

Blessed is the congregation that insists that believers gather to worship God not, first of all, in order that God might bless them, but because God has already blessed them.

Blessed is the congregation that then discovers that God does indeed bless them as they worship the triune God who nourishes, teaches, convicts, and corrects them, and strengthens bonds that unite believers with Jesus Christ and with each other through the sanctifying actions of the proclamation of the Word and corporate prayer, through baptism and the Lord's Supper, through fellowship, offerings, and testimony.

◐ Easter Sunday morning, 2008, in a village church in China

Taken seriously, these first four proverbs alone would be enough to rock the world of many contemporary worshipers. This is especially the case in North America where, nurtured by a consumer culture, people have come to believe that if they choose to worship God at all, it is because they have taken the initiative. "God should be pleased that we have made that choice," they think. How ironic that people would consider worshiping the triune God and yet be self-absorbed!

To quote C.S. Lewis, "like an ignorant child who wants to go on making mud pies in a slum because he cannot imagine what is meant by the offer of a holiday at the sea," (*The Weight of Glory*, The Macmillan Company, 1949, p. 2), we can easily miss the astonishing truth that God is deeply invested in a relationship with us. The Creator of every universe that has ever existed revealed himself to us in Jesus Christ; the Spirit who hovered over precreation chaos is the same Spirit that drags us out of bed (or out of ourselves) and into a posture of praise.

TESTIMONY

"Every Sunday is received with expectation. We begin with something like, 'We have been called by God today to. . . .' And then the joy inside of us bursts out and we begin our worship in song. We cannot worship God only with our heads and with our arms folded. Praise, for us, is the physical expression of our gratitude."

—*Eduardo Gonzales, Tegucigalpa, Honduras*

God created us to worship. Worship is our home, praise is our voice, and prayer is the air our lungs were designed to breathe! God calls us to worship and makes our worship possible. We do not love, serve, or worship God in order to attract his attention, avoid his wrath, or secure his blessing. God, in Jesus Christ, has come to us, redeemed us, and blessed us. It's a done deal. Worship is a "sacrifice of praise"—our grateful response to these blessings.

Questions for Reflection:

1. Why might those who are intentional in worship be "blessed?" What helpful parallels can you draw between these proverbs and Jesus' teaching in the Beatitudes (Matt. 5:3-12)?

2. How does your congregation gather? How would a visitor describe the spirit of the gathering? Would it be clear that you gather in response to God's invitation, with joy for what God has already done?

3. As your congregation gathers for worship, how do you celebrate the great reality of

- ■ God's splendor and majesty?

- ■ God's perfect revelation in Jesus Christ?

- ■ God's activity as the Holy Spirit moves through the congregation?

1.2 Corporate Assembly—the Whole People of God: Who Gathers?

Wise is the worshiping community that "does not neglect meeting together" (Heb. 10:25), but joyfully gathers in Jesus' name, eager to proclaim the Word of God, to offer praise and prayer, and to celebrate the sacraments, each of which are actions of the whole people of God, "the royal priesthood" (1 Pet. 2:9).

Blessed is the congregation that invites all worshipers—including those which our cultures may label in different ways as "disabled"—to full, conscious, and active participation in corporate worship, engaging heart, soul, and mind in devotion to God, deeply aware of how their own personal worship participates in a much larger chorus of praise to God.

Blessed is the congregation that expresses in its worship the communion in the body of Christ, the unity of the Spirit in the bond of peace, and the oneness that is the gift and calling of God that unites the young and old and believers of every time and place who share a common calling by the Spirit of God in Jesus Christ.

← Praising God in Pakistan

→ Worship in a poor village in Pakistan

↑ Bangladeshi Christians praising God in worship

As important as the "why" of worship is the question of "who" shows up; what attitudes, expectations, and hopes do we bring with us?

If we center our hearts on the person and work of Jesus Christ, eagerly proclaiming God's Word and joyfully celebrating the sacraments, we create a countercultural community—a gathering of uncommon joy, compassion, and welcome. Does this describe your congregation, or do you long for worship that offers something more? Passionate worship, inspired by the Holy Spirit and oblivious to the demon of self-consciousness, is something that disciples of Jesus in the West can learn from our sisters and brothers in other parts of the world. But learning to worship with freedom from cultural constraints takes wisdom. It is here, at the beginning of section 1.2 of "Worshiping the Triune God," that wisdom joins the conversation.

Wisdom—as distinct from knowledge, regulation, tradition, formula, or even "blessing"—is what gives disciples of Jesus the ability to flourish regardless of their circumstances. A congregation is wise to make joy-infused worship the center of their life together. The discipline of regular worship is where disciples are nurtured, spiritual growth and life transitions are marked, and the "royal priesthood" of God's people is both formed and strengthened.

Such a wise congregation will be blessed all the more as they recognize and encourage the many and varied gifts and talents of their "priests." But many contemporary people have become accustomed to "professional" leadership. They are content to be the recipients of professionally produced sporting and entertainment events and discriminating consumers of professionally franchised merchandise. It's not a stretch, then, for people who come to the "worship event" to leave leadership and even active participation to "professional" worship leaders and to be underwhelmed, if not somewhat embarrassed, by home-grown expressions of praise, prayer, or proclamation. But there is great blessing in allowing the dialect of our community to become the language of our worship, and encouraging the particular gifts of those gathered for worship to shape our corporate encounter with the triune God.

When a worshiping community is drawn lovingly and persistently into active participation, worship can arise more naturally from every heart, mind, and tongue; from young and old; rich and poor; men and women; in word, song, image, sign, and posture. And when attention is paid to people with special giftedness and/or special needs, the grace-filled embrace of the triune God is extended, and the Holy Spirit will most certainly provide unexpected blessings.

"Our Freewill Fellowship has been growing steadily from a small group of physically and /or mentally handicapped brothers and sisters to about 300. From young to old, they attend fellowship and worship services with the help of many devoted volunteers. They are usually the most enthusiastic participants in the worship services! Their choir occasionally sings in the worship services; their heartfelt singing is way too beautiful to imagine. Hallelujah! We are blessed and completed by their presence and testimonies."

—*Yvette Lau, Hong Kong*

Questions for Reflection

1. Participating in "the unity of the Spirit through the bond of peace" (Eph. 4:3) is a significant goal for the witness of the twenty-first-century Church around the globe. What is the basis of the unity expressed in section 1.2? How can we more closely achieve this kind of unity through our worship?

2. What special gifts might people who have disabilities bring into a worshiping community? In what ways might they experience and share a rich relationship with the triune God?

3. What "disabilities" do you personally bring to your participation in worship?

4. In what ways is your congregation encouraged to be good hosts to visitors, especially those perceived as being "different"?

1.3 The Holy Spirit: "Who" Else Is There?

Wise is the worshiping community that recognizes how the Holy Spirit works through both reason and emotion, through both spiritual disciplines and surprising events, through both services that are prayerfully planned and through moments of spontaneous discovery.

Wise is the worshiping community that recognizes that the lasting value or spiritual power of worship does not depend upon our own creativity, imagination, intellect, or emotions, but comes from the Holy Spirit, who may choose to use any or all of these things. For, truly, worship is a gift to receive, not an accomplishment to achieve.

". . . Worship is a gift to receive, not an accomplishment to achieve." This one sentence, and the proverb containing it, provides the wisdom that signals a non-negotiable cease-fire to the unfortunately named "worship wars" many have endured. The Holy Spirit can and may choose to work through the head, the heart, the body, the rehearsal, the "accident," the prayer book, the spontaneous intercession, the organ, the drums, the banners, the lights, the hymnals, the screen . . . or none of the above.

Questions for Reflection

1. How broad and welcoming is your congregation's experience of worship? Where do you see the most evidence of the Holy Spirit at work in the life of your worshiping community?

2. Individual disciples of Jesus are unique. In the same way, every gathering of worshipers develops its own "personality." How does your congregation balance careful preparation with spontaneity, attempting to reach both the head and the heart of worshipers?

3. Where might the Holy Spirit be challenging you to grow in your experience of the fullness of the gospel as it is embodied in worship?

Prayer

God of all time, Father, Son, and Spirit,
in every generation you call people to worship,
inviting, inspiring, and instructing;
naming, nourishing, and nurturing;
uniting us with one another and with you.
Thank you for the gift of worship.
We pray for your wisdom
so that we may receive your blessings
with a full and grateful heart.
May all we say and do bring glory to you
and shalom to a shattered world.
We pray in the name of Jesus. Amen.

PHOTO BY PAUL DETTERMAN

⬆ Aboriginal church choir festival in Changhua, Taiwan

➲ Tech room in a large Hong Kong church

Session 1-B: Going Deeper

A song from Zimbabwe

Jesu, tawa pano;	Jesus, we are here;
Jesu, tawa pano;	Jesus, we are here;
Jesu, tawa pano;	Jesus, we are here;
tawa pano mu zita renyu.	we are here for you.

A song from England

Angels, help us to adore him;
you behold him face to face.
Sun and moon, bow down before him,
dwellers all in time and space.
Alleluia, Alleluia!
Praise with us the God of grace!

A song from Taiwan

萬民啊，恁當讚美，	Let all nations praise the Lord,
恁當讚美主上帝；	and all people bless God's name,
伊對咱大施慈愛，	for God's faithfulness and love
伊信實到萬世代。	are forever firm and sure.

God's Word commissions disciples of Jesus to be "in" the world—aware of the world's questions and suffering, contributing to the world's beauty and art, modeling the highest and best ethics, morals, and standards of citizenship. But Scripture is equally clear that, while the church has a place in the world, there are many aspects of the world that have no place in the church.

When it comes to living out this distinction, worship is one of the most important filters.

What are the people in your congregation doing during the week? What are they watching, reading, absorbing from conversations? How are they making use of media and the Internet? What voices are inside their heads? What shapes their expectations and defines their hopes and dreams? How much time and energy do they spend working too hard to "get ahead," or playing too hard to "get away from it all"? How much time do they spend in Scripture and prayer during the week, as individuals or in families?

The answers to questions like these will define the intersection of the worshiping community and the surrounding culture—where life encounters the gospel.

In this context, conversations in the twenty-first century "across continents and centuries" become very interesting. In many places, disciples of Jesus are being nourished in astonishingly vibrant Christian communities. New worshiping congregations are forming, new believers are being baptized and welcomed into a life of radical faith, the fruit of the Spirit is evident, and signs and wonders of the kingdom of God abound.

In other places around the world, however, faith in Jesus Christ has been dismissed as a shallow myth or identified as a catalyst for persecution. In still other cultures, significant generational and cultural tensions abound as the influence of Christianity is being rapidly replaced by religious pluralism (different faith systems regarded with equal weight and importance) and a postmodern allergy to absolute truth. But the church, the body of Christ, has always existed across and among differing cultures, and has always faced the competition and confrontation of other value systems.

As we discussed earlier, we bring our context with us. Our experience of life will always be a combination of good and evil. "The dissonance of evil persists right through the harmony of praise, and is not easily resolved. Nobody who goes to church leaves the memory of evil outside the door. . . . All creation, says the apostle Paul, awaits the day when it 'will be set free from its bondage to decay and will obtain the freedom of the glory of the children of God' (Rom. 8:20-21)" (Cornelius Plantinga, Jr. and Sue A. Rozeboom, *Discerning the Spirits*, Eerdmans, 2003, p. 141).

Worship is the place where the lure of our culture encounters the power of the triune God to overcome the dissonance outside (and, at times, within) the church. Says C.S. Lewis, "[Humanity] can no more diminish God's glory by refusing to worship Him than a lunatic can put out the sun by scribbling the word 'darkness' on the walls of his cell" (*The Problem of Pain,* Macmillan, 1962, p. 53).

Questions for Reflection

1. How would you describe the dominant cultural influences in your congregation, and how are they the same as or different from the culture influencing your community?

2. How are these cultural influences changing? Is your congregation responding to these changes? If so, how? If not, why not?

3. Does your congregation encourage expressions of joy and sorrow during worship? How are such expressions received?

1.4 Affirming and Resisting Culture: What Shapes Our Worship?

Wise is the church that seeks to be "in" but not "of" the world (John 15:19), resisting aspects of the culture that compromise the integrity of the gospel, and eagerly engaging its culture with the good news of the gospel of Jesus Christ who comes to each culture but is not bound by any culture.

Wise, then, is the church that is grateful that the gospel of Jesus is at once transcultural, contextual, cross-cultural, and counter-cultural.

⊙ Indonesian liturgical dance for the opening song in worship.

← Traditional instruments speak of Indonesia's heritage and are used in outreach to the Batavian people.

→ An Indonesian congregation accompanies singing on occasion with gamelan instruments to honor their cultural heritage.

← Traditional Indonesian drums to accompany singing

→ Traditional and modern Indonesian musicians lead worship together.

Unconditional love and forgiveness, the promise of grace, and transformation through relationship with the triune God know no limitations of gender, race, age, orientation, or ethnicity. As cross-cultural mission workers know, people who have experienced transformative faith in Jesus Christ through the language of one culture can often have serious difficulty unraveling their experience of the triune God from the language, customs, images, and expectations of that nurturing culture.

Hymn writers and musicians in parts of Asia, for example, have encountered much resistance to indigenous worship music because it is different from the nineteenth-century gospel hymns Western missionaries brought with them. At the same time, worshipers in the West have often resisted receiving the gifts of song that now are available from our brothers and sisters in other parts of the world. And any congregation with a healthy balance of old and young worshipers knows the challenge of interweaving the worship music of different generational "cultures."

The good news of Jesus Christ, and worship centered around that good news, is not bound by any one culture's words or music, postures or prayer. Opportunities to experience authentic Christian worship from a totally different culture can provide that "You too?" moment when the living Christ unites his people in praise.

As part of the one body of Christ, both within your local congregation and around the world, disciples of Jesus are called to seek unity with the mind and heart of Jesus that transcends cultural and generational differences. But such unity does not imply uniformity. The words "transcultural, contextual, cross-cultural, and countercultural" describe an ideal of worship for any congregation. These four visionary words come from a document you may wish to explore further (see box).

Worship of the triune God will always be contextual. But drawing on the rich tapestry that is the body of Christ around the globe, vibrant worship also transcends, utilizes, and challenges the expectations, resources, and preferences of any one "culture" to receive and respond to the good news of the Savior.

Nairobi Statement on Worship and Culture

Christian worship relates dynamically to culture in at least four ways, according to a helpful document prepared in 1996 by a study team representing five continents, gathered in Nairobi, Kenya by the Lutheran World Federation. Christian worship is called to be transcultural, the same substance for everyone everywhere, beyond culture; contextual, varying according to the local situation; countercultural, challenging what is contrary to the gospel in a given culture; and cross-cultural, sharing and receiving gifts from the larger church to honor the unity of the body of Christ. For the full text of the Nairobi Statement, see www.worship.ca/docs/lwf_ns.html.

Questions for Reflection

1. What cultures are represented in your congregation? (Every congregation has more than one!)

2. How is your congregation engaging these cultures in your worship?

3. How do the songs you sing in worship provide examples of what is transcultural, contextual, countercultural, and cross-cultural?

1.5 The Goodness of the Redeemed Creation: Where Worship Connects with Creation

Wise is the congregation that makes clear that its worship participates in the song of praise that is offered by all creation.

Wise is the congregation that celebrates worship as an embodied reality, grateful for the gestures and postures that express our praise and prayer, and the book, water, bread, and wine that God ordains for our use—the gifts of God for the people of God.

Another reality of worship named earlier was, "'logging on' to the unending worship of the triune God across creation and throughout time." Scripture promises that God's whole creation is being redeemed and prepared for the time when "the earth will be filled with the knowledge of the glory of the Lord" (Hab. 2:14) and

◉ Indonesians
sing with
enthusiasm!

when "the mountains and hills will burst into song" and "all the trees of the field will clap their hands" (Is. 55:12). Our worship should give us a taste of that cosmic worship to come, in effect becoming a rehearsal of the kind of worship that one day we will fully engage in with all of creation.

Questions for Reflection

1. In what ways does the worship in which you participate most clearly join in the praise of the whole creation?

2. What does it mean to you that worship is "embodied reality"? What aspects of the worship life of your community help you understand this?

1.6 Leading God's People: When Leadership Is Leadership

Wise is the community that calls, trains, affirms, and responds to those gifted for leadership in all genders, ages, races, and abilities, providing formative training and mentorship for them in the theology and practices of worship.

Wise are leaders in worship who equip all the members of the community for full, conscious, and active participation (cf Vatican II) taking care to express hospitality to those who are not yet a part of Christ's body, the church.

We have already considered the wisdom and blessing of recognizing and encouraging the varied gifts and talents within any congregation or worshiping community. However, simply identifying spiritual giftedness is not sufficient preparation for worship leadership. In order to move beyond common expectations of worship leaders, it can be helpful to turn the phrase around: think of them as "lead worshipers."

The distinction is not a play on words. It challenges what a worshiping community expects of those who guide worship and how people are nurtured to fulfill that expectation. There is a tangible difference between people who are trained to "perform" and those who are freed to "lead by worshiping." But this freedom can require as much of a change in the heart and preparation of the leaders as it does in the mind and expectation of the congregation. Let's explore several dimensions of this distinction.

"Worship leaders" may be professional speakers or musicians, or they may be congregation members who have been asked to "do something" in worship. Defaulting to the role of a group facilitator in the secular world, these leaders may assume a position of authority in the eyes of the worshiping community and read or play what they have prepared (or what has been prepared for them) with the goal of moving the congregation through their part of the "agenda" of the worship service.

"Lead worshipers," on the other hand, may be professionals or congregational peers, but they are called first of all to be worshipers, joining their gifts with everyone else in a common offering of praise. They prepare the worshiping community to encounter the triune God, creating the expectation of interaction, conversation, and response to God, and then stepping back into the community to share in that encounter.

"Worship leaders" emerge from a culture in which performance superstars dominate media and performer "wannabes" inundate YouTube and talk radio. "Lead worshipers" must be coached to be as countercultural as the act of worship itself. They must understand the words, phrases, gestures, and rituals of worship; be encouraged to hone their gifts through practice and review; and be offered opportunities for continuing growth and experience so they can serve God with personal integrity and encourage authentic response from others. Training lead worshipers requires a substantial investment of time, effort, vision, and passion. It is its own form of discipleship.

Questions for Reflection

1. Who are the leaders of worship in your community? (Think carefully and broadly—you might be surprised by your answer!)

2. Do the people leading worship reflect the diversity of your worshiping community?

3. How are the people who lead worship in your community identified, trained, and nurtured?

4. Using the distinctions above, are your worship leaders "lead worshipers"? Why or why not?

1.7 Artistic Expression

Blessed is the congregation in which the Word is proclaimed and prayers and praise are offered not only through words, but also through artistic expression: through gifts God has given to each local community in music and dance, in speech and silence, in visual art and architecture.

Blessed are the artists who offer and discipline their gifts so God's people may testify to the goodness of God, offer thanks, and express repentance.

Wise are artists who are grateful both for the limitations offered by the second commandment, and also for the example of the biblical artists called by God and equipped by God's people for service according to God's commands (Ex. 35:30ff).

Wise is the church that gratefully receives the gifts of faithful songs and artworks from other centuries and other cultures, celebrating the catholicity of the church and cultivating creativity through new songs and works for worship.

Visual arts and music, speech and dance—all can be offered in the service of worship. They are God's gifts, evidence of natural ability combined with training and practice. Used wisely and well, they can point us toward the triune God, the one and only object of our worship. Artists, writers, and performers who contribute to the worship of God's people allow worshipers to reach through them and their media to connect with God.

A dancer in Jamaica in a joint worship service on Ash Wednesday, a national holiday in Jamaica

Indonesian/Chinese fan dancers participate in morning worship.

Dancing during singing in Mizoram, India

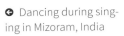

A Swiss organ in a Japanese Reformed Church

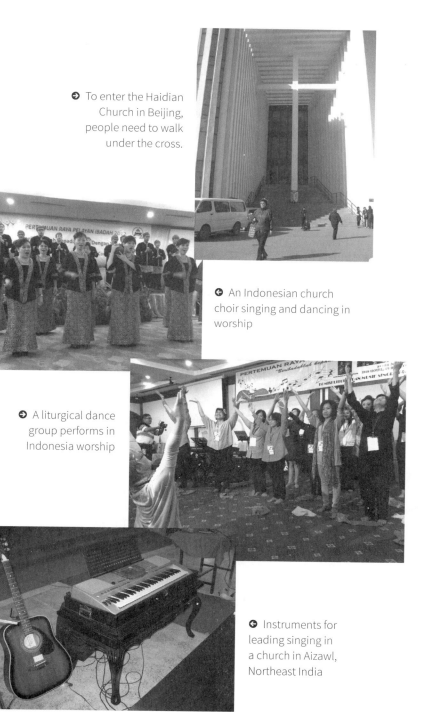

➔ To enter the Haidian Church in Beijing, people need to walk under the cross.

◀ An Indonesian church choir singing and dancing in worship

➔ A liturgical dance group performs in Indonesia worship

◀ Instruments for leading singing in a church in Aizawl, Northeast India

But disciples of Jesus have a further role in the world of the arts. We who worship the triune God also have a biblical obligation to ensure the protection and proliferation of beauty. Throughout much of its history, the Church has been the curator of the arts, often commissioning artists and musicians to communicate biblical truth and catechize new believers. This opportunity continues today with new technologies and emerging media. As Quentin Schultze writes, "Worship is meant to be artfully done, with respect for what is good, true, and beautiful—even what is pleasing to the senses" (*High-Tech Worship?*, Baker Books, 2004, p. 36). Here too, the conversation "across continents and centuries" can become particularly interesting.

As inheritors of millennia of Judeo-Christian art, we have the opportunity to explore the richness of that heritage in our twenty-first-century worship, limited only by our imagination and our ability to interpret the artistic praise from other continents and centuries to our local worshiping community.

Questions for Reflection

1. How does your congregation value and nurture the arts in worship through music, words, visual images, dance, drama? Do you use the gifts of people in your own community (children as well as adults) and the gifts of people across the world? How?

2. What are some barriers to welcoming deep artistic expression in worship?

3. How does your congregation nurture beauty in worship? Have you ever commissioned an artist for a specific work of music, an image, a dance, or a drama? Is your worship space itself a place of beauty?

4. What could your worshiping community help create that would not only deepen your corporate experience of the triune God in worship but also communicate the good news of Jesus Christ into the world around you?

Prayer

Creator God, Author of life and of new life in Christ,
we acknowledge that every culture finds a way
to vandalize your creation and reject your will.
And yet, your patient love endures.
Open our eyes to recognize your beauty
and our arms to welcome all people.
Inspire us to be artists, each in our own right,
reflecting the light and life of Jesus Christ
into the dark and defiant places of our world,
beginning in our own hearts.
We ask this in Jesus' name. Amen.

The Risen Lord, by He Qi, China. www.heqigallery.com. Used by permission.

Session 2: Proclamation

A song from Ireland and England

Speak, O Lord, as we come to you
to receive the food of your holy Word.
Take your truth, plant it deep in us;
shape and fashion us in your likeness—
that the light of Christ may be seen today
in our acts of love and our deeds of faith.
Speak, O Lord, and fulfill in us
all your purposes for your glory.

Teach us, Lord, full obedience,
holy reverence, true humility.
Test our thoughts and our attitudes
in the radiance of your purity.
Cause our faith to rise; cause our eyes to see
your majestic love and authority.
Words of power that can never fail;
let your truth prevail over unbelief.

Speak, O Lord, and renew our minds;
help us grasp the heights of your plans for us.
Truths unchanged from the dawn of time
that will echo down through eternity.
And by grace we'll stand on your promises,
and by faith we'll walk as you walk with us.
Speak, O Lord, till your church is built
and the earth is filled with your glory.

Nothing else in all creation rivals the power of God's Word. God spoke, and an ordered universe emerged out of chaos, containing levels of intricacy, beauty, and wonder that the greatest minds can never fully comprehend and the most skilled artists can never duplicate. God spoke, and an entire nation was released from tyrannical oppression. God's Word became flesh: his Son became Savior, his Light became life, and darkness and death were destroyed forever.

Yet, some will ask, in cultures defined by ten-second commercial spots, texting, tweeting, and multitasking, can the reading of an ancient text and the exploration of its teachings remain significant to God's people? Yes! God's Word changes lives.

As Lukas Vischer writes,

> Holy Scripture, the written Word of God, bears witness to Jesus Christ, the living Word of God, and so is at the center of all areas of life in the Reformed tradition, including its worship. Scripture points to Christ as the authority by which the church assembles in the name and presence of the triune God. . . . Scripture leads the church to confess its sins in penitence and faith, to hear that its sins are forgiven, to give praise and thanksgiving in prayer and song, to intercede for the church and the world, and to celebrate baptism and the Lord's Supper" (*Christian Worship in Reformed Churches Today*, Eerdmans, 2003, p. 288).

The writer of Psalm 119 calls God's Word "a light to [our] path" (119:105, NRSV). The apostle Paul, arrested for proclaiming the good news, rejoiced; because of his imprisonment, the prison guards were being converted (Phil. 1:12-14). Protestant reformers in the sixteenth century identified the proclamation of God's Word as the first mark of the true church. Centuries later, the United Presbyterian Church in North America identified "the proclamation of the gospel for the salvation of humankind" as the first of six "great ends" (ultimate purposes) of the Church.

The act of proclamation, whether through music, images, other forms of the arts, or speech, creates the intersection where the power of God's Word encounters the lives of God's people. While all of worship is proclamation, there should always be a time designated for extended exploration and "unpacking" of particular portions of Scripture. Thoughtful worship is designed to prepare our hearts first to receive and then to respond to God's Word proclaimed.

Session 2-A: Let's Talk

A song from Germany

All our knowledge, sense, and sight
lie in deepest darkness shrouded,
till your Spirit breaks our night
with your beams of truth unclouded.
You alone to God can win us;
you must work all good within us.

From: "Blessed Jesus, at Your Word"
Words: Tobias Clausnitzer, 1663; tr. Catherine Winkworth, 1858, alt., P.D.

A Kiowa song

Dawk'yah towgyah
thawy báhtawm.
Dawk'yah towgyah
thawy báhtawm.
Dawk'yah towgyah
thawy Gyah O' Boy Daw.

Take the saving
Word of God;
put it first within
your life.
Nothing comes before
God's Holy Word.

From: "Dawk'yah towgyah/Take the Saving Word of God"
Words: Pawltay (Kiowa); English vers. John Thornburg, English vers. © 2008 General Board of
Global Ministries t/a GBGMusik, 475 Riverside Drive, New York, NY 10114. All rights reserved.

2.1 Word and Spirit

Blessed is the congregation in which the Word of God is proclaimed with conviction and joy, surrounded by expectant prayers and profound gratitude for the Holy Spirit's work to illuminate the hearts and minds of God's people.

As with any other act of worship, the dialogue of proclamation begins through God's initiative—God's Word comes to us. Only through God's provocation can we respond to the Word with conviction and joy, and only through the proclamation of God's Word that changes lives can we begin to relate to one another as disciples of Jesus.

⬆ Attentive in worship at Chilgal Church, Pyongyang, North Korea

PHOTO BY MARILYN BORST

⬆ Listening to God's Word in Cambodian Fellowship Church

⬅ Bringing God's Word in song in Hong Kong

We receive the gift of God's Word. (↓)

We respond by offering our lives to God. (↑)

We allow God's Word to shape our relationships with others. (↔)

Throughout Scripture, we see a repeated pattern. God commissioned Jeremiah (↓) to be "a prophet to the nations," saying, "I have put my words in your mouth" (Jer. 1:5, 9). Jeremiah responded, proclaiming God's truth to his struggling people, and shepherding them (↔) through captivity and exile with the promise of restoration and a new covenant.

Ezekiel received an even more interesting charge. God instructed him (↓) to "eat this scroll; then go and speak to the people of Israel" (3:1). Ezekiel faithfully proclaimed God's truth to a despondent, exiled people, keeping alive their faith in God's presence and the promise of God's redemption (↔).

In Jesus Christ, God took the ultimate initiative. The Word of God "became flesh and made his dwelling among us. We have seen his glory, the glory of the one and only Son . . . full of grace and truth" (↓) (John 1:14). As disciples of Jesus we hear God's Word proclaimed and respond in faith (↑) through commitment to lives of obedience, selflessness, and humble service (↔). God commissions us to "show that [we] are a letter from Christ . . . written not with ink but with the Spirit of the living God, not on tablets of stone but on tablets of human hearts" (2 Cor. 3:3).

Careful proclamation of God's Word amplifies this give-and-take: God's action, our response, and our unity with one another as we seek the mind of Christ (Eph. 5:1). Every time we worship, rehearse, remember, and renew our participation in God's covenant, the rhythm of proclamation forms the heartbeat for all other aspects of worship. And, like a composer creating a symphony from one simple musical idea, the Holy Spirit uses the heartbeat of worship to create the "phrases" and "movements" of daily existence until our life becomes a "symphony of praise" glorifying and enjoying the triune God, as the Westminster Shorter Catechism states in question 1. The prayer for illumination, asking the Spirit to aid the reading, hearing, and preaching of God's Word, reminds us that God, unseen but very active, is always at work.

Questions for Reflection

1. How do you recognize and how would you describe "conviction and joy" in the proclamation of the Word of God?

2. Is the reading of Scripture something to which you look forward with anticipation? In what different ways are different types of Scripture presented with imagination and conviction?

3. Does your congregation include a prayer for illumination in worship? If not, what are some other ways you are helping worshipers be receptive to the proclamation of God's Word?

A traditional Hasidic song

Open your ears, O faithful people,
open your ears and hear God's Word.
Open your hearts, O royal priesthood,
God has come to you.

God has spoken to the people, hallelujah!
God has spoken words of wisdom, hallelujah!

They who have ears to hear the message,
they who have ears, now let them hear.
They who would learn the way of wisdom,
let them hear God's Word.

From: "Open Your Ears, O Faithful People"
Words: Hasidic traditional; tr. Willard F. Jabusch © 1966, 1982 Willard F. Jabusch, admin. OCP Publications, 5536 NE Hassalo, Portland, OR 97213. All rights reserved.. st. 3, Psalm 78:4, vers Martin Tel © 2011 Martin Tel, admin. Faith Alive Christian Resources

A song from the United States

In vain we search for meaning
where transient joys abound;
and seek the soul's contentment
where peace cannot be found.
We wander, lost and homeless,
in endless, aimless quest,
our hearts forever restless,
until in you they rest.

From: "Cast Down, O God, the Idols"
Words: Herman G. Stuempfle (1923-2007) © 1997 GIA Publications, Inc., 7404 S. Mason Ave. Chicago, IL 60638. www.giamusic.com, 800.442.1358. All rights reserved. Used by permission.

2.2 The Breadth of the Christ-Centered Word

Wise is the congregation that nourishes believers with readings and sermons that engage the breadth and depth of God's Word, Old Testament and New Testament, always proclaiming the fullness of the gospel of Jesus Christ.

2.3 Calling Forth Rest and Witness, Justice and Peace

Blessed is the congregation in which the proclamation of God's Word comforts those who mourn and confronts those who oppose God's reign.

Wise is the preacher who invites hearers to receive God's lavish grace, to repent from sin and evil, to turn toward Christ, to proclaim peace, "to do justice, to love kindness and to walk humbly with God" (Mic. 6:8).

◒ The chapel at the Presbyterian retreat center near Alexandria, Egypt

◒ Lectern, pulpit, and table in Mizoram, India

◑ Worship leaders in Pakistan singing the psalms

◑ Haidian Christian Church, Beijing, China

↑ Reading God's Word in Nepal

◑ Chinese choir members taking notes during the sermon

It is relatively easy to chart the conversation between God and God's people throughout the flow of worship.

- God calls us to worship (↓) and we respond (↑), often inviting the world to join us in praise and adoration (↔).

- God calls us to holiness (↓); we confess our sin (↑) and are assured of God's forgiveness and grace (↓). We cry "Gloria!" in gratitude (↑) and remember God's Law as the revelation of his will for human thought, action, and relationships, and we seek God's peace and reconciliation with one another (↔).

- God calls us to be attentive to his Word (↓). We pray for the presence of God's Spirit and listen carefully, not for teaching about God's Word, but for the Word itself (↑), which draws us closer to Christ and unites us to one another. Shaped by God's Word, we profess our faith with disciples of Jesus across continents and centuries (↔).

- God provides for all our needs: family, friends, relationships, beauty, work, material possessions (↓). We respond with adoration, thanksgiving, and intercession (↑), uniting our hearts in compassionate care and stewardship for one another and for all who are "our neighbors" (↔) (Luke 10:25-37).

- God calls us to the font and to the table (↓). We respond as individual disciples (↑) joined in a worshiping community (↔) committed to nurturing those who seek to grow in faith and to joyfully proclaiming Christ's victory over death until he returns.

- God calls us to leave our "sanctuary" and face the challenges and the opportunities of bold discipleship in his world (↓). We respond (↑) by striving to live transformed lives amid the idols and temptations of a fallen world, and by praying for one another and holding each other accountable for our words and our actions, constantly seeking God's justice and peace. (↔)

In his letter to the believers in the region of Galatia, the apostle Paul wrote, "If anyone is preaching to you a gospel other than what you accepted, let them be under God's curse!" (Gal. 1:9)—to which John Calvin commented, "Let us bear in mind that the one who is speaking is not doing so by his own authority, but in the name of Jesus Christ" (*Sermons on Galatians*, Old Paths Publications, 1995). The power of preaching is not found, first of all, in the preacher, but in the power of God.

Disciples of Jesus can easily forget the dynamic power contained in the Word of God. Like an ordinary driver behind the wheel of a Lamborghini, we don't always know what to do with the power available to us. In many congregations, God's story is simply retold each year in a predictable series of readings and festivals. Life goes on.

N.T. Wright puts the same thought another way. Reflecting on Trinity Sunday, the Sunday after Pentecost that focuses on the majesty and the mystery of the triune God, he writes:

> In the church's year, Trinity Sunday is the day when we stand back from the extraordinary sequence of events that we've been celebrating for the previous five months—Advent, Christmas, Epiphany, Lent, Good Friday, Easter, Ascension, Pentecost—and when we rub the sleep from our eyes and discover what the word "god" might actually mean. These events function as a sequence of well-aimed hammer-blows which knock at the clay jars of the gods we want, the gods who reinforce our own pride or prejudice, until they fall away and reveal instead a very different god, a dangerous god, a subversive god, a god who comes to us like a blind beggar with wounds in his hands, a god who comes to us in wind and fire, in bread and wine, in flesh and blood; a god who says to us, "You did not choose me, I chose you."
> —*For All God's Worth*, Eerdmans, 1997, p. 24.

This dangerous, subversive, triune God is revealed in the full breadth of Scripture. When Scripture is proclaimed in its fullness, we become even more aware that God meets us in the darkest corners of our distress and simultaneously defeats the power of death itself. God's Spirit, who moved through predawn creation, who conceived the Savior in Mary's womb, who fell upon the disciples at Pentecost, is at this moment invading your thoughts and directing your consideration of this very sentence. If that unsettles you just a little, you're beginning to understand God's subversive abilities!

When Scripture in its fullness is proclaimed and applied to the life of a worshiping community, that congregation will become increasingly eager disciples of Jesus Christ, not just people of the New Testament alone, but people of the whole Book, from Genesis to Revelation and everything in between. Scripture is not an anthology of sixty-six different short stories. God's overarching story can be traced throughout Scripture. Because all of worship is a form of proclamation, Scripture can appear in different forms.

Worship in the Reformed tradition ordinarily begins with the words of Scripture, either from the psalms or from other biblical invitations to praise.

The psalms are God's gifts to us to offer back in prayer and praise; hymn texts and other worship songs can also be based on Scripture, and certainly should be deeply rooted in Scripture.

Scripture readings can offer the greatest opportunity for immersing worshipers in God's Word, especially when more than one passage of Scripture is read in preparation for preaching and when passages from the Old as well as the New Testament are regularly included for reading and preaching.

The invitation to the Lord's Supper comes directly from Scripture. When the full text of the Great Prayer of Thanksgiving is prayed, biblical accounts of the Father, Son, and Holy Spirit are often included in this profession of Christian faith.

The "call to discipleship" (words of challenge) and "blessing" (God's good word to us of assurance and covenant) at the close of worship often incorporate Jesus' words of commission and promise.

When worship is thoughtfully designed and intentionally led, mature disciples of Jesus can be nurtured, new believers can be strengthened, those who come questioning can be catechized, skeptics can be challenged, and everyone present can experience the dynamic beauty of God's Word.

While the different books of the Bible give different points of entry into the great covenant story of God's creation and the redemption of us and our world, there are, as Tim Keller has said, "only two questions to ask. . . . Is [Scripture] about me or about Jesus? Is the Bible basically about what I must do or about what [Jesus] has done?" (taken from *Center Church: Doing Balanced Gospel-Centered Ministry in Your City* by Tim Keller, p. 79. Copyright © 2012 by Redeemer City to City and Timothy J. Keller. Used by permission of Zondervan. www.zondervan.com).

As many who will use this study know, the Heidelberg Catechism begins with that question and offers this answer: ". . . I am not my own, but belong—body and soul, in life and in death—to my faithful Savior Jesus Christ." The second question of the Catechism asks, "What must you know to live and die in the joy of this comfort?" and the answer is important in framing our understanding of proclamation: "Three things: first, how great my sin and misery are; second, how I am set free from all my sins and misery; third, how I am to thank God for such deliverance."

Proclamation of the fullness of God's Word, encased in the worship of the triune God, grounds our core identity in Jesus Christ, nurtures knowledge and commitment to discipleship, and creates an environment of grace, selflessness, and joy that ultimately propels disciples into the world to fulfill Christ's commission.

Proclamation for Gospel Renewal

Tim Keller identifies five characteristics of preaching that help bring about gospel renewal. These same five points apply equally well to all forms of proclamation.

1. Preach to distinguish between religion and the gospel.

Effective preaching . . . will address the core problems of idolatry by helping listeners look beneath the level of behavior to their hearts' motivation.

2. Preach both the holiness and the love of God to convey the richness of grace. . . .

Only when people see God as absolutely holy and absolutely loving will the cross of Jesus truly electrify and change them.

3. Preach not only to make the truth clear but also to make it real. . . .

Preaching must not simply tell people what to do. It must re-present Christ in such a way that he captures the heart and imagination more than material things.

4. Preach Christ from every text. . . .

There are, in the end, only two questions to ask as we read the Bible: Is it about me? Or is it about Jesus? In other words, is the Bible basically about what I must do or about what he has done?

5. Preach to both Christians and non-Christians at once. . . .

Evangelize as you edify, and edify as you evangelize.

—taken from *Center Church: Doing Balanced Gospel-Centered Ministry in Your City* by Tim Keller, pp. 77-79. Copyright © 2012 by Redeemer City to City and Timothy J. Keller. Used by permission of Zondervan. www.zondervan.com.

Questions for Reflection

1. Do you approach worship expecting to be changed? Why or why not?

2. Are you experiencing the delight the Holy Spirit can bring? Are you experiencing refreshment from the proclamation of God's Word?

3. Think back to your most recent experience of worship. Where, and in what different ways, did you hear Scripture used and God's Word proclaimed?

4. In what ways is the proclamation of God's Word essential to supporting the mission of Jesus' disciples in our daily lives?

5. How has your congregation encouraged young people to study God's Word in order to develop their gifts as artists, musicians, poets, or preachers? How have you used those gifts in worship?

Prayer

Eternal, triune God,
your Word is unchanging and yet always new.
Comfort us with your presence,
confront us with your truth,
and compel us to embody the gospel we receive
in acts of justice and kindness,
in words of hope and compassion,
and in lives of humble service.
All this we ask in Jesus' name. Amen.

Session 2-B: Idol Thoughts and Strong Beliefs

A song from England

Just as I am, though tossed about
with many a conflict, many a doubt,
fightings and fears within, without,
O Lamb of God, I come! I come!

From: "Just as I Am, Without One Plea"
Words: Charlotte Elliot, 1836, P.D.

2.4   Resisting Idolatry

Wise is the congregation that proclaims the Word of God in ways that actively expose and resist both the idols that we are tempted to worship instead of God and also the idols of our distorted understandings of God.

Blessed is the congregation that challenges these distortions by contemplating the person and work of Jesus Christ, "the radiance of God's glory and the exact representation of God's being" (Heb. 1:3).

⬆ Young Ethiopian men singing a song written for worship based on a tune traditionally sung when men were going off to war against their enemies. They retained the tune, but they wrote new words for it that talk about our battle with Satan and the need to be vigilant and to engage in the power of God.

These proverbs, like many in this conversation, focus on the worshiping congregation as a whole—the community that together exposes and undermines idolatry, and together unmasks our distortions of God by discovering the reality of Christ. Personal spiritual discipline can deepen our knowledge of Scripture and strengthen our commitment to love and obey Jesus Christ. It takes a worshiping community working together, however, to represent the complex, multifaceted nature of the triune God and to unmask and challenge distorted interpretations of God's will and purpose.

Idolatry is a subtle sin. It can mask itself with chameleon-like ease, often masquerading as a worthy goal or a great ambition. Our best and most laudable intentions can easily become objects of idolatry if they are allowed to displace God as our ultimate desire.

Tainted with sin and vulnerable as we are, we can even distort our understanding of God to match our personal aims and ambitions. When we catch ourselves saying, "The God I know would never ask me to sacrifice that . . ." or "Surely God would never want me to move there . . ." or "I can't imagine God would ever allow me to lose him/her . . ." we are in danger of worshiping a god we created in our image, not the triune God who created us in his.

Scripture is crucial to maintaining that perspective. Tod Bolsinger observes:

> Writers have penned many words more beautiful and inspirational than "love bears all things." Nevertheless, we want [1 Corinthians 13] read at our weddings. Why is that? Because part of us knows that there's enough emotion in the room already, and that we need to be reminded of what true love is and what marriage requires. Amid all [the] wedding sentimentality, 1 Corinthians 13 is read so that we will remember it after the wedding, when we need to be reminded that love is going to endure all things, including you.

—*It Takes a Church to Raise a Christian*, Brazos Press, 2004, p. 116.

Questions for Reflection

1. Can you name some idols or distorted understandings of God in the worship life of your congregation?

2. What does God's Word say about those particular idols?

3. Does your congregation include confession of sin as a regular part of worship? Is confession always used in the same way, or does your worship community have different ways of inviting worshipers to confess distortions of God, God's will, and God's purpose?

4. What does it mean to you that our Savior is "the radiance of God's glory and the exact representation of God's being"? How would you "proclaim" that biblical truth in your own words?

2.5 Credo: The Response of Faith

Wise is the congregation in which the proclamation of the gospel is accepted as the Word of God, which is at work in you who believe (1 Thess. 2:13), leading to both confession and praise, both repentance and a commitment to service, both compassion and a passion for justice, both personal and communal actions, both new obedience and profound gratitude.

Blessed is the congregation that invites believers to testify to the goodness of God by expressing the faith of the church that transcends and forms our individual experiences and unites us with believers across cultures and centuries, and by testifying to the work of God in the life of the local community.

Nothing else in all creation rivals the power of God's Word. When God's Word is proclaimed, it bears fruit: lives are changed. As disciples of Jesus, we have the unique privilege of actively anticipating those changes, beginning within ourselves.

God's Spirit, at work through proclamation, frees us to confess our sins readily, receive God's grace with gratitude, and worship the triune God with the joyful abandon of people unburdened from our most crippling disabilities. God's Spirit, prompting our response to proclamation, can turn our hearts from selfish ambition to passionate service of others, seeking God's justice and peace. God's Spirit, revealed in proclamation, enables us to discover the blessings of following Jesus, expressing deep gratitude for all God has done (Heidelberg Q&A 2) and living each day with contagious joy.

All of worship is enacted proclamation that leads to transformation. John Witvliet makes these observations:

> We hear repeated references—and perhaps an occasional explanation, of the Trinity, but we also experience prayer offered to the Father through the Son, in the Spirit—prayers that invite us to imagine God as the One who is before us, alongside us, and within us. We hear the claim that Jesus is God's Son, who became human for our salvation. But we also practice this claim when we take bread and wine that are provocatively given to us as "the body and blood of Jesus. . . ."

> Through the lens of worship, all the idolatries of money, sex, and power—even if only in a momentary glimpse—are put in their proper place. . . .

> The melodies, rhythms, and harmonies of worship evoke and shape certain emotions in us. They may allow us to experience grandeur or gratitude or lament in ways that will happen in no other part of our lives—affections that, because they are offered in the name of God, become permanently attached in our minds and hearts with our notion of God and true spirituality. . . .

> Worship enacts a conversation between God and the gathered community. We learn to hear God speak words of comfort, assurance, challenge, and correction. We speak words of praise, lament, gratitude, and confession. . . .

> Worship forms us to consider each other as brothers and sisters in Christ, regardless of age, gender, race, or socioeconomic class. Worship forms us to act toward each other as fellow servants, as fellow saints in patterns of interaction that do not come naturally to us in any walk of life.

> In a culture of self-centeredness, worship is one of the few activities whose intrinsic purpose is to "decenter"

ourselves, to see what it feels like not to be the center of the universe in which we live.

—"The Cumulative Power of Transformation in Public Worship" in *Worship that Changes Lives,* Baker Academic, 2008, pp. 49-50

TESTIMONY

The architects of the Pniëlkerk (see Gen. 32:30) had in mind the picture of Jesus teaching on the mountain with people gathered around him, sitting on the slopes. The ceiling is blue and white for sky and clouds and set with small lights like stars for use at night. The most striking feature is the unique central light fixture. From a central sphere sixty antennae reach out, with lights at the end of each. The antennae are from army vehicles; swords made into plowshares. The message is for the church to be an antenna sending peace into the world. Each member is called to "be an antenna for the peace-bringing Word of God."

The Pniëlkerk in Utrecht, the Netherlands

As we worship the triune God, we not only proclaim and embody God's Word within the context of our culture, we join present-day disciples of Jesus across continents and saints across twenty previous centuries in experiencing and embodying faith in Jesus Christ. Nowhere is this more evident than when we speak one of the great creeds of the Church. As Ron Byars writes,

The creed is not the possession of any single individual; it belongs to the church catholic, to the covenanted community, called and chosen at God's initiative. . . . As individuals, any one of us would likely choose to articulate the doctrinal content of our faith in words that are particularly appropriate to us. We would choose words that express our experience, our history, our particular ways of speaking. But when the church is summoned to rise and profess its common faith, it does so not in a cacophony of simultaneous personal testimonies, but in words that belong to the community of saints, including both the living and the dead. Just as we do not each invent our own words to the hymns we sing in church but sing texts that express faith, perhaps, quite differently than we would do if left to our own devices, we profess the faith of the church with one voice because we are part of the church.

—"Creeds and Prayers = Ecclesiology" in *A More Profound Alleluia,* Eerdmans, 2005, p. 89

Questions for Reflection

1. How can you encourage people in your worshiping community to actively and eagerly look for the "fruit" of the proclamation of God's Word?

2. How often do you recite one of the ecumenical creeds together? If you don't do so every Sunday, how and why do you choose to recite a creed?

3. In what ways do you see faith as part of something larger and more transcendent than personal expression or experience?

Prayer

Loving God,
we can so easily become distracted and deceived,
believing we are worshiping you
when we are giving our hearts to lesser gods.
Through the preaching of your Word,
the power of your Spirit,
and the witness of your Church,
draw us back to you,
proclaiming your truth and your grace
in all we say and do.
We pray this in Jesus' name. Amen.

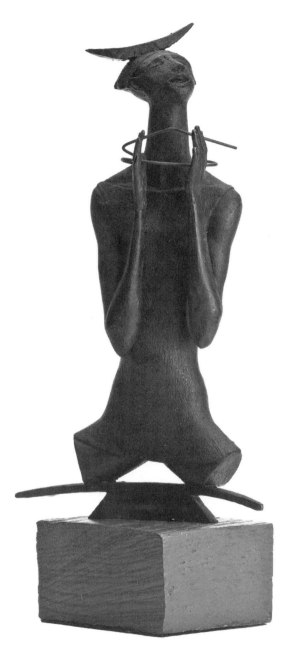

⬆ *Praise IV,* by C. Malcolm Powers. Used by permission.

Session 3: Prayer and Offering

A song from the United States

At the crossroads of decision
Wisdom calls to all and each:
"Come, my children, learn and listen—
heed the ways I seek to teach."
Conscious thoughts or intuition
frame her words of grace and peace:
"Choose the pathway of the Lord."

On the ash heap of disaster
"Where is God?" we cry and weep.
Friends are false and faith uncertain;
Wisdom seems beyond our reach.
Still she whispers from the whirlwind
of our pain and of our grief,
"Trust the goodness of the Lord."

On a cross and in a manger
God's compassion is made plain.
"Word made flesh" is God among us;
"He is risen"—hope for pain.
"Come, you weary," pleads the Savior;
Wisdom calls to us again:
"Cast your burdens on the Lord."

From: "Wisdom Calls"
Words: Carol Bechtel © 2012 Carol Bechtel, admin. Faith Alive Christian Resources

In the covenantal conversation of worship, it is now the congregation's turn to "speak." God has spoken to us through his Word. Now we respond in prayer and self-giving. The response we begin in corporate worship will continue throughout the coming week. For as surely as God calls us together, he also sends us out in much the same way that Jesus was led by the Spirit into the desert to be tempted (Matt. 4:1-11), and the disciples were led by Jesus from the mountain of the Transfiguration into the valley where a little boy was waiting to be healed (Matt. 17:1-21).

What has your day been like? Have you been praying through the day? Have your responses to people and situations been shaped by blessing or stress? Have you been conscious of God's presence in your conversations, God's leading in your decisions, and God's grace and protection in your relationships, or have you been so focused on simply getting through the day that you need to make a deliberate effort to realize how close God is to you at this very moment? Now think back to last Sunday's worship. What words, images, thoughts, and actions prepared you for today's challenges?

Prayer in response to God's Word enlarges the heart of individual disciples and forms the passion and soul of a worshiping community. Listening to and participating in prayers voiced on our behalf enables us to look beyond ourselves, seeing God's world from a different perspective and living into that difference. Through prayer we can praise God, even in challenging circumstances; thank God for beauty and joy, even in dismal places; question God about things that confuse or confound us; cry out to God in frustration, anger, or fear; and bring to God the burden we feel for the needs of others.

The offering of ourselves through gifts of money and service is another way in which our hearts can be enlarged and joy can be increased. Giving our tithes and offerings in corporate worship not only teaches us the blessing of generosity, but also helps us maintain a biblical perspective on God's provision and a faithful relationship to material possessions. Generosity practiced as part of a worshiping community will eventually enable us to be truly selfless in every other part of our individual lives.

Session 3-A: Praying Well with Others

A song from the United States

He came to live, live a perfect life;
he came to be the living Word, our light.
He came to die so we'd be reconciled;
he came to rise to show his power and might.

That's why we praise Him, that's why we sing.
That's why we offer him our everything.
That's why we bow down and worship this king,
'cause he gave his everything.

He came to live, live again in us;
he came to be our conquering King and Friend.
He came to heal and show the lost ones his love;
he came to go prepare a place for us.

From: "That's Why We Praise Him"
Words: Tommy Walker © 1999 Doulos Publishing/We Mobile Music, admin. Music Services, Inc.

3.1 Praise and Gratitude

Blessed is the church that offers praise and thanksgiving (cf Ps. 50:14, Heb. 13:15), not only extolling the beauty and glory of God, but also contemplating, reciting, and celebrating all that God has done throughout history.

Wise is the congregation that draws upon and learns from the Bible's own narratively-shaped prayers of praise and thanksgiving (e.g. Ps. 136) as it gives form to its own prayer.

As we mentioned earlier, Christian worship is simultaneously contemporary and eternal—informed by the moment and rooted in history. Wonderful as it is to praise God for the beauty of any given day, it becomes an amazing and humbling blessing to realize that we are, in that moment, worshiping the Creator of every beautiful day that has ever existed. God who inspires us to sing also unleashed the angels' festival chorus at the creation of the

➔ Choir in Nepal leading the congregation in prayer

◉ Leading the singing with guitar, harmonium, and tabla in Bangladesh

world and the incarnation of his Son. We are part of something much larger than we realize!

Not surprisingly, Scripture helps us gain perspective on this bigger picture. No matter what opportunities or challenges we face, God and God's people have "been there before." We can learn how to live faithfully in our current circumstances by praying with disciples of Jesus from other times and situations. When we pray, we are, to a certain extent, lip-synching with Abraham and Sarah, Moses and Miriam, Hannah, David, Isaiah, Mary, and thousands of other women and men who comprise the "great cloud of witnesses" (Heb. 12:1), God's faithful people throughout time.

Questions for Reflection

1. Where have you seen the beauty and glory of God revealed today? Have you made the effort to consciously respond with praise and thanksgiving?

2. Why is praising God often referred to as a "sacrifice?" (Heb. 13:15) What is meant by "the fruit of lips that openly profess his name"?

3. Read Psalm 136 and notice the narrative of God's power and love at work in the recital of God's dealings with the people of Israel. Does any similar narrative of your own congregation or your own life help you pray with a similar recital and response because "his love endures forever"?

Christ, to you, with God the Father
and the Spirit, there shall be
hymn and chant and high thanksgiving
and the shout of jubilee:
honor, glory, and dominion
and eternal victory evermore and evermore.

From: "Of the Father's Love Begotten"
Words: Marcus Aurelius Clemens Prudentius (348-413); tr. Composite, P.D.

3.2 Praying in Jesus' Name, through the Spirit

Blessed is the church that prays in Jesus' name, acknowledging our union with our ascended and ever-present Lord.

Blessed is the worshiping community that prays in and through the Holy Spirit, desiring the gifts of the Holy Spirit, and acknowledging that as we pray the Holy Spirit helps us in our weakness, interceding for us according to the will of God (Rom. 8:26, 27) and resisting the "cosmic powers of this present darkness" (Eph. 6:12).

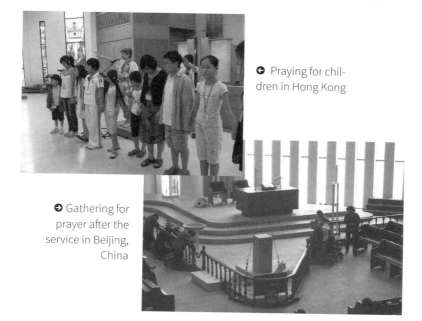

○ Praying for children in Hong Kong

➔ Gathering for prayer after the service in Beijing, China

71

As disciples of Jesus we worship the triune God; Father, Son and Spirit, united as one. Because of Jesus, we can offer our prayers to God, the Creator of heaven and earth. Because of Jesus, we can call this cosmic God "our Father" (Matt. 6:9). Because we are united with Christ, we who are sinful can experience the intimate love and unconditional acceptance of God, who is both holy and just. As the Heidelberg Catechism states in Q&A 37,

> During his whole life on earth, but especially at the end, Christ sustained in body and soul the wrath of God against the sin of the whole human race. This he did in order that, by his suffering as the only atoning sacrifice, he might deliver us, body and soul, from eternal condemnation, and gain for us God's grace, righteousness, and eternal life.

Scripture is filled with the blessings of union with Christ. Among these are the presence and power of the Holy Spirit, our Intercessor, Advocate, Counselor, and Comforter. To turn the proverb from "Worshiping the Triune God" around, "Impoverished is the worshiping community that does not pray in and through the Holy Spirit, afraid of the gifts of the Spirit, failing to acknowledge that as we pray the Holy Spirit helps us in our weakness. . . ." We are often content to "shoot a few prayers up to God now and then," never realizing the blessing of an intimate, ongoing relationship with the living God.

A correct understanding of the nature of prayer to our triune God has implications for how we begin and end those prayers. Scripture uses a wide range of names for God, and it would be helpful to address God with a full range of biblical imagery in worship (for a helpful list, see *The Worship Sourcebook*, Faith Alive, 2004, pp. 178 ff). When we end our prayers "in the name of Jesus" we acknowledge that it is our Savior who will bring our prayers before the Father.

Questions for Reflection

1. Locate passages of Scripture that mention "union with" or "being united with" Christ. What promises do they list?

2. What are some ways that we acknowledge our union with Christ in prayer? What happens when you offer the same prayer omitting that acknowledgment? Read Romans 8:26-27. What

does it mean that "... we do not know how to pray as we ought" (NRSV)? What are some of the things people in your worshiping community may be "sighing" for?

A song from the United States

Lᴏʀᴅ, I bring my songs to you,
every day declaring praise.
All the meek shall hear my words
always telling of your ways.
Join with me your heart and voice
praise the Lᴏʀᴅ, in him rejoice.

From: "Psalm 24, Lord, I Bring My Song to You"
Words: Marie J. Post, 1985, © 1987 Faith Alive Christian Resources

A song from the United States

Lying lips that falsely flatter
keep the truth far out of reach.
Come, O God, and still the chatter;
end their boasts and twisted speech.

From: "Lying Lips"
Words: Adam M. L. Tice © 2011 GIA Publications, Inc.

⬅ Psalm and hymn board, Delft Oude Kerk, the Netherlands

3.3 Full Range of Human Experience

Wise is the church that, following the example of the psalms, encourages honest and trusting prayers to God that express the full range of human experience—the "anatomy of the soul"—spoken, sung, or silent, danced, dramatized, or visualized—prayers of celebration and lament, trust and desperation, supplication and intercession, thanksgiving and confession, healing and hope.

Blessed is the church that prays not only for its own needs, but also for the needs of the world that God so loves.

Careful reading—and praying and singing—of the psalms proves nothing is off-limits in conversation with God! John Calvin described the psalms as "the anatomy of all parts of the soul." He wrote, ". . . there is not an emotion of which any one can be conscious that is not represented [in the psalms] as in a mirror. . . . The heart is brought into the light, purged from that most baneful infection—hypocrisy" (from Calvin's preface to his *Commentary on the Psalms*). Achieving and maintaining that level of honesty with God is one of the blessings and one of the goals of worship.

TESTIMONY

Psalm 18 is the most popular psalm in Pakistan. It represents God's providence, safety, power, deliverance, and kindness. In our context of living below the poverty line and facing discrimination and hard challenges every day, it gives hope and encouragement. The majority of people in village congregations are illiterate and speak only Punjabi. They love to sing psalms of praise, laments, penitence, petitions, and prayers. They memorize them by heart. Only two or three persons in my congregation can read, so the Punjabi *Zaboors* [Psalms] is their Bible. It helps them in their daily life, especially when they face questions from Muslims in their workplaces.

—Eric Sarwar, Pakistan

There are countless ways that a worshiping congregation can pray together. Most congregational singing is prayer; and the way songs are introduced helps the congregation to understand that they are called to pray as they sing. Involving the congregation in spoken prayer through brief responses, spoken or sung, helps to keep everyone fully engaged in prayer, not simply listening to someone else. The "amen" (literally, "so be it!") said at the end of the prayer blends everyone's voice with those who have prayed out loud. The "amen" is meant to be said communally. A common practice in China is for everyone to say "amen" at the end of every sentence!

A variety of people can lead the prayers of the worshiping community. Some congregations delegate this prayer to their pastor, who knows the congregation well. Others are blessed by recognizing the gifts of a variety of people, each bringing their own voice, life experience, and passion to the community's prayer. No matter how we pray, it is easy to overlook or undervalue the work of God's Spirit, missing the deep delight of being honest with "our Father" about the things that matter most in our lives, singing and dancing and playing before God, laughing or weeping or admitting (out loud) that we are hurt or perplexed.

In some cultures, freely expressed response to God can be diminished by a self-conscious fear of what others will think. Only when we begin to present our own lives to God in communal prayer can we begin to know the blessing of being fully engaged in voicing the needs of others. In response, as in so many other acts of worship, we need help and encouragement from sisters and brothers around the world who are less inhibited than we.

TESTIMONY

What do I know without ambiguity after my years of worshiping with African Christians? They pray. They pray standing up, they pray moving around, they pray kneeling down, they pray in loud voices, they pray all night. African Christians believe in the efficacy of prayer, join it with regular and intense fasting, and offer their lives to a God who hears and acts. Life is about prayer, and prayer is life. Prayer is theology lived, embodied, and enacted in daily life.

—*Mark R. Gornik, in* Word Made Global: Stories of African Christianity in New York City, *Eerdmans, 2011, p. 127*

Questions for Reflection

1. What are some of the different ways your worshiping community prays?

2. Are there emotions or topics that are, intentionally or unintentionally, "off limits"? Why?

3. How are you nurturing prayerful attention to the needs of the world God loves?

◐ The deacons' room just off the platform, Binhai Church, Shandong Province, China

➲ Offering of music in Singapore

◐ Dancing to bring offerings forward in the Sunyani Presbyterian Church, Ghana

3.4 Gifts and Offerings

Wise is the church that gratefully practices the giving of gifts, time, and talent as an act of dedication and worship.

Wise is the church which affirms that all of life is lived in service to God and neighbor, and that believers are called to be stewards of every gift of God.

Most people think of money when they hear the word "offering." In corporate worship, however, "offering" is a verb. Gifts of love and charity, including money, may be received during the service. But as an offering in response to God's Word, a choir may sing a beautiful anthem, a child may play a simple hymn, or an artist may display a visual interpretation of Scripture or the sermon. As an act of self-giving, worshipers can take a request for a particular need in the community from the offering basket or donate food for the local food bank or school supplies for community children. In other worshiping communities, testimonies are offerings, thanking God for the assurance of his presence or for answered prayer.

There is no such thing as a selfish Christian. Although many selfish, self-focused, and self-centered people may claim to be disciples of Jesus, Scripture reminds us repeatedly that Jesus came to serve, not to be served, and this is to be the pattern of life for his followers as well. As disciples of Jesus, we offer our whole selves—money, yes, but also time, ability, attention, attendance, intelligence, expertise—as a gift of thanksgiving to God. And the ninety percent we do not tithe directly to God, we are called to offer in service to others. This is the response: worship—a gospel-shaped life.

On the Sunday closest to Epiphany, every congregation in the Evangelical Presbyterian Church in Egypt gathers a "Bethlehem's Baby gift" for the denomination's hospitals, clinics, schools, and social service and employment agencies. These gifts to social justice causes help us remember the gifts of the magi to the infant Christ. We follow their model in presenting our gifts to all who don't receive a proper welcome and honor in our society.

—*Anne Zaki, Egypt*

Prayer

> Just and holy God,
> you need nothing from us,
> but delight in our humble trust
> and grateful obedience.
> Save us from shallow prayers
> and empty acts of giving.
> Meet us in our deepest need.
> Open our eyes to the needs of others,
> and our hearts to be generous
> with all we have received from you.
> We ask this in Jesus' name. Amen.

Session 3-B: Prayer and Self-Giving in Daily Life

As we consider now the second avenue of response to God's Word—prayer and self-giving in the worship that is our daily life—the challenge and opportunity increases exponentially. While there are some generalities in our vocation of daily worship (the importance of time spent in prayer and the study of God's Word, the joy of teaching children and new believers the stories of Jesus, the practice of generous hospitality, and the need for spiritual accountability) there is no prescribed method, no "suggested order of worship," for the daily life of a Christian. But the call is clear: every moment of every day we are called to respond in obedience to God: at home, at school, at work, in our government, and in every relationship we have.

To guide this section of our conversation we offer a few psalms, hymns, and spiritual songs, as well as some of the proverbs from the previous section, but we'll focus here on our individual responses through daily worship. Pray through these texts alone, and then discuss them as a group, perhaps singing them together as well.

3.1 Praise and Gratitude

Blessed is the church that offers praise and thanksgiving, not only extolling the beauty and glory of God, but also contemplating, reciting, and celebrating all that God has done throughout history. . . .

Read or sing Psalm 104 from a Bible or hymnal; this psalm is wonderfully pictorial, able to delight both adult and child.

Read or sing the following song from the United States.

> This is my Father's world,
> and to my listening ears
> all nature sings, and round me rings
> the music of the spheres.
> This is my Father's world;
> I rest me in the thought
> of rocks and trees, of skies and seas—

his hand the wonders wrought.

This is my Father's world;
the birds their carols raise;
the morning light, the lily white,
declare their Maker's praise.
This is my Father's world;
he shines in all that's fair.
In the rustling grass I hear him pass;
he speaks to me everywhere.

This is my Father's world;
Oh, let me not forget
that though the wrong seems oft so strong,
God is the ruler yet.
This is my Father's world;
why should my heart be sad?
The Lord is King, let the heavens ring!
God reigns, let the earth be glad.

From: "This Is My Father's World"
Words: Maltbie D. Babcock (1858-1901), P.D.

Questions for Reflection

1. Where do you see God's ongoing involvement in his creation?

2. What does it mean to you to "rest in the thought" of God's created wonders?

3. In what tangible ways can the promise of God's continuing presence strengthen you when "the wrong seems so strong?" What is the best way for you to share this assurance with others who are facing difficult struggles?

3.2 Praise and Gratitude

. . . Blessed is the worshiping community that prays in and through the Holy Spirit, desiring the gifts of the Spirit, and acknowledging that as we pray the Holy Spirit helps us in our weakness, interceding for us according to the will of God, and resisting the "cosmic powers of this present darkness. . . ."

Read Luke 4:14-21 and Matthew 5:3-12.

Read or sing the following song from the United States:

A song from the United States

Arise, your light is come!
The Spirit's call obey;
show forth the glory of your God
which shines on you today.

Arise, your light is come!
Fling wide the prison door;
proclaim the captives' liberty,
good tidings to the poor.

Arise, your light is come!
All you in sorrow born,
bind up the broken-hearted ones
and comfort those who mourn.

Arise, your light is come!
The mountains burst in song!
Rise up like eagles on the wing;
God's power will make us strong.

From: "Arise, Your Light Is Come"
Words: Ruth Duck, 1974, © 1992 GIA Publications, Inc., 7404 S. Mason Ave., Chicago, IL 60638
www.giamusic.com. 800.442.1358. All rights reserved. Used by permission.

Questions for Reflection

1. How did God's glory shine on you today?

2. What various forms of "captivity" are people you know experiencing? What would God's promise of release mean to them?

3. Read Matthew 5:11-12 and stanza 4 of the hymn. What is God saying to you today?

3.3 Praise and Gratitude

. . . Blessed is the church that prays not only for its own needs, but also for the needs of the world that God so loves.

Read Matthew 9:35-36 and Jeremiah 29:4-7.

Pray by reading or singing this song from the United States:

The city is alive, O God,
with sounds of hustling feet,
with rapid change and flashing lights
that pulse through every street;
but oft there's inhumanity
behind the bright facade,
and throngs with empty, hungering hearts
cry out for help, O God.

Is it your will, O loving God,
that races live in strife?
That loneliness and greed and hate
should mark a city's life?
Do you desire one person's wealth
to keep another poor?
Must crime and slums, and lust abound?
O Lord, is there no cure?

In Galilee the people heard
your servant Christ declare
through healing touch, through word and cross,
the good news of your care.
He said your heart touched every heart
that longed for peace and right,
that those bowed down by burdens borne
could find your life, your light.

O God, inspire your church today
to take Christ's servant role,
to love the world, to hear its claims
to sense its yearning soul,
to live within the marketplace,
to serve both weak and strong,
to lose itself, to share the dream,
to give the world its song.

From: "The City Is Alive, O God"
Words: William W. Reid Jr, alt. © 1969 The Hymn Society, admin. Hope Publishing Company, Carol
Stream, IL 60188. All rights reserved. Used by permission.

Questions for Reflection

1. What do you hear in this text? What parallels can you draw between the hymn and the description of Jesus' ministry in Matthew 9?

2. This hymn is a prayer of lament. The first two stanzas plead with God to change the circumstances the poet is observing. The final two stanzas hold out gospel hope. Where do you see yourself in this text? How might this be your lament?

3. Where are the places in your community to which you can take the "word and cross," the good news of Jesus Christ, in very practical ways?

3.4   Praise and Gratitude

. . . Wise is the church that affirms that all of life is lived in service to God and neighbor, and that believers are called to be stewards of every gift of God.

Read Luke 5:1-11 and Matthew 5:13-16.

Read or sing this song from Scotland:

> Will you come and follow me, if I but call your name?
> Will you go where you don't know and never be the same?
> Will you let my love be shown,
> will you let my name be known,
> will you let my life be grown in you, and you in me?
>
> Will you leave yourself behind, if I but call your name?
> Will you care for cruel and kind and never be the same?
> Will you risk the hostile stare
> should your life attract or scare?
> Will you let me answer prayer in you, and you in me?
>
> Will you let the blinded see, if I but call your name?
> Will you set the prisoners free and never be the same?
> Will you kiss the leper clean,
> and do such as this unseen,
> and admit to what I mean in you, and you in me?

Will you love the "you" you hide, if I but call your name?
Will you quell the fear inside and never be the same?
Will you use the faith you've found
to reshape the world around,
through my sight and touch and sound in you, and you in me?

Lord, your summons echoes true when you but call my name.
Let me turn and follow you and never be the same.
In your company I'll go where your love and footsteps show.
Thus I'll move and live and grow in you, and you in me.

Questions for Reflection

1. Discipleship, the commitment to hear and answer the call of Jesus, is always costly. What would the commitment to follow Jesus "in service to God and neighbor" cost you?

2. What part of you do you hide from God? How would you describe "the fear inside," and how can you use the tools of daily and communal worship to address that fear?

3. What does a "gospel-shaped" life mean to you? How would your daily life need to change in order to be a "steward of every good gift of God"?

Prayer

Ever-present God, Father, Son, and Spirit,
because of your great love for us
you have created this world.
Out of that same great love
you shape and guide each moment of every day.
How can we do anything but give you glory
and give ourselves joyfully in your service?
We thank and praise you in Jesus' name. Amen.

⬆ *The River* by Elizabeth Steele Halstead, United States. Reprinted by permission from "Visuals for Worship" © 2006 Faith Alive Christian Resources.

Session 4: Baptism and the Lord's Supper

A song from the United States

Wash, O God, our sons and daughters,
where your cleansing waters flow.
Number them among your people;
bless as Christ blessed long ago.
Weave them garments bright and sparkling;
compass them with love and light.
Fill, anoint them; send your Spirit,
holy dove and heart's delight.

We who bring them long for nurture;
by your milk may we be fed.
Let us join your feast, partaking
cup of blessing, living bread.
God, renew us, guide our footsteps,
free from sin and all its snares,
one with Christ in living, dying,
by your Spirit, children, heirs.

Oh, how deep your holy wisdom!
Unimagined, all your ways!
To your name be glory, honor!
With our lives we worship, praise!
We your people stand before you,
water-washed and Spirit-born.
By your grace our lives we offer.
Recreate us: God, transform!

From: "Wash, O God, Our Sons and Daughters"
Words: Ruth Duck (b. 1947) © 1989 The United Methodist Publishing House, admin. The Copyright Company, Nashville, TN. All rights reserved. International copyright secured. Used by permission.

4.1 Jesus' Commands to Baptize and Celebrate the Lord's Supper

Blessed is the church that faithfully obeys Jesus' commands "to make disciples, baptizing them in the name of the Father, Son, and Holy Spirit and teaching them to obey everything [Jesus has] commanded" (Matt. 28:20) and to "eat and drink in remembrance of me" (Luke 22:19-20), receiving these signs as occasions in which God works to nourish and sustain, comfort and challenge, teach and transform us.

PHOTO BY MARILYN BORST

➊ Communion at the Presbyterian church in Damascus, Syria

➋ A communion service in Jamaica on Ash Wednesday, 2012

At this point in our conversation on worship, we shift our focus from words to actions. As the Heidelberg Catechism observes in Q&A 66, the sacraments of baptism and the Lord's Supper are "visible, holy signs and seals. They were instituted by God so that by our use of them he might make us understand more clearly the promise of the gospel, and seal that promise. And this is God's promise: to grant us forgiveness of sins and eternal life by grace because of Christ's one sacrifice accomplished on the cross."

In the Reformed tradition, God's Word and the sacraments are united as one. John Calvin wrote, "First, the Lord teaches and instructs us by his Word. Secondly, he confirms it by the sacraments. Finally, he illumines our minds by the light of his Holy Spirit and opens our hearts for the Word and sacraments to enter in . . ." (*Institutes of the Christian Religion*, 4.14.8)

Put another way, to the extent that we believe what we have heard through proclamation and mean what we have prayed, the baptismal font becomes a visual reminder of the covenant God has made with us and the commission we have received to share God's promise with the eager expectation that people will hear and receive it for themselves. Likewise, the communion table takes on new meaning as we celebrate, with eager joy, Christ's victory over death and his promised return. At the table we get to hear the salvation story told once more and join in shouting our acclamation on cue: "Christ has died! Christ is risen! Christ will come again!"

Do you see the font and the table this way? Always having the font and table present in worship, even if we don't celebrate the sacraments weekly, is a good visual reminder. If they're not permanent fixtures, their occasional presence may signal that worship is about to run long. Sacraments, viewed pragmatically, become "problems" to be "solved." People request a baptism. This is a problem because our "normal" worship already fills the hour. When can we squeeze this in? Communion takes time, so we sometimes say, "Keep the singing short and cut down the preaching. We can't let the service run too long."

The story is told of a traveler who stopped to gaze across the beautiful Yosemite Valley in California. He was admiring God's creation, awed and amazed by the beauty of waterfalls, lakes, and the giant sequoia trees, when he overheard a person near him saying, "You know, if they dammed that lake and flooded this valley, they could irrigate most of the farms in central California." The analysis was probably correct, and the motivation behind the thought was probably admirable, but the person speaking saw only the means to solve a problem, not the beauty of God's creation.

Thankfully, there are those who thrill to the sacrament of baptism, in which God makes promises to new members of God's covenant, and in which they remember their own promises to participate in God's mission. And there are those who are hungry to be fed at the table, eager for communion with their Lord after hearing the Word proclaimed. How can that grateful eagerness be nurtured throughout your congregation? That is the focus of this session.

Session 4-A: You Have Put on Christ

A song from Latin America

Todos los que han sido bautizados
han sido revestidos en Christo Jesús,
han sido revestidos en Christo Jesús.

Que el Espíritu Divino
nos dirija y dé sostén
en la lucha por la vida
y nos guíe hasta el Edén.

All who have been baptized in Christ Jesus
have also been re-clothed with our Lord Jesus Christ,
have also been re-clothed with our Lord Jesus Christ.

Holy Spirit, lead and guide,
sustain us through each day of life
till we gather in the new creation,
face to face with Christ.

From: "Todos los que han sido bautizados/All Who Have Been Baptized"
Words: Fernando Rodríguez © 1989 OCP Publications; adapt. Emily Brink © 2008 Faith Alive
Christian Resources. OCP Publications, 5536 NE Hassalo, Portland, OR 97213. All rights reserved.
Used with permission.

4.2   Baptism

Blessed is the congregation that announces that their true identity is found in Jesus Christ.

Blessed is the congregation that proclaims how the waters of baptism are a sign and seal of God's promises to wash us clean, to adopt us into the body of Christ, to send the Holy Spirit to renew, empower, and resurrect us to new life in Christ.

Blessed is the congregation that proclaims how the waters of baptism are also a sign and seal of God's call to renounce sin and evil, to embrace Christ and our new identity in him, and to live a renewed and holy life.

Wise is the community that celebrates baptism joyfully and re-members that baptism is a means of grace and encouragement to live out our vows of covenant faithfulness.

PHOTO BY PAUL DETTERMAN

◑ Baptismal font with water is present at every service in the chapel of the Taiwan Theological College and Seminary in Taipei.

◑ A Syrian Orthodox baptismal font in Aleppo, Syria

People who attend worship regularly see many baptisms, if their congregation is blessed with young families and if their work in evangelism has brought new youth and adults into the fellowship of believers. In the Reformed tradition, the vast majority of those receiving baptism are infants or young children.

The sacrament of baptism is packed with significance and joy, and our celebration must ensure that the following list gets our attention. Baptism

- announces our identity in Jesus Christ, the Savior of the world.

- proclaims the great promises of God, the Creator of all, who cleanses us from sin, saves us from eternal death, and claims us as his own.

- anoints children and new believers with the power of God's Holy Spirit.

- invites everyone present to reaffirm their own commitments to renounce the power of sin and evil, embrace Christ, and reclaim a transformed life.

That list is significant indeed! Baptism calls for careful preparation and joyful celebration. Putting this list at the center will help when we're tempted to turn baptism into a (biological) family celebration observed by the congregation.

During the Cultural Revolution in China, all churches were closed from 1966 to 1978, and all religions—not just Christianity—were banned. This was a period of great pain and suffering for the Chinese people. When the ban was finally lifted, thousands of people turned to Christ and to the church—and continue to do so by the millions, in a most remarkable story of God's faithfulness to the Chinese people. As a result, Chinese churches experience many baptisms.

In many countries, baptism is accompanied by testimony of faith and transformation, evidence plainly spoken of God's power, grace, and tenacious love. We who are witnesses to this sacramental reality, and who by our presence and vows are pledging our continuing participation in the covenant that is being formed before our eyes, also need to realize that God is doing amazing things in our midst!

As Marion Clark writes,

> Baptism is not the act by which a convert comes before God and says, "I want to give you a sign that I have now decided to be identified with you." Nor is it an opportunity for parents to let God know that they will raise their child for him as best they can. No, God calls forth the person whom he has regenerated, saying, "Here is my sign to you that I have decided to identify you with me. Here is my sign to you that I have already baptized you through the Holy Spirit." To parents [God] is saying, "Bring your child to me. Here is my sign to you that your child belongs to me."

—"Baptism and the Joyful Sign of the Gospel" in *Give Praise to God*, P&R Publishing, 2003, p. 178

Meeting with church leaders after a service in a church in Shanghai, I learned that they had about 300 baptisms last year, celebrated near Christmas and near Easter, some in morning, some in evening services, about sixty at a time. Inquirers study Scripture and other materials for several weeks in preparation. The next week, meeting with church leaders of a congregation in Beijing, I mentioned that figure. Their response was: "Only 300?"

—*Emily Brink, 2007 diary*

When we witness a baptism, we are not only seeing visible evidence of human response to God's initiative, the pattern that defines all of our worship, but we become participants in God's covenant with the new believer, no matter what that person's age may be. Baptism marks the beginning of a life of obedience and discipleship. God has claimed the person being baptized, calling them "out of darkness and into his wonderful light" (1 Pet. 2:9). All disciples of Jesus who witness the baptism are drawn into God's covenant as we promise to nurture, encourage, and pray for the new believer, becoming a significant part of their "family" with all the rights and responsibilities of family membership. We join with God—Father, Son, and Holy Spirit—in surrounding and sustaining fellow disciples, celebrating their joy, consoling them in their sorrow, and challenging them to active participation in God's mission.

As Philip Butin observes,

> If Trinitarian faith is about God's identity, then our shared baptism in the strong name of the Trinity is ultimately about our identity as God's people. That identity, that confidence of *who we are*, grows out of our conviction and experience of *Whose we are*. We are baptized. Our triune God holds us firmly and securely in the divine embrace. We are baptized. Our identity is constituted by our relationships with God and one another in the baptismal community, the church. We are baptized. In life and in death, we belong—not to ourselves—but to God who proved faithfulness in raising Jesus from the dead by the power of the Spirit.

—*The Trinity*, Geneva Press, 2001, pp. 117-18

Martin Luther, one of the great sixteenth-century reformers, routinely fought off the temptations of the devil by growling, "I HAVE BEEN BAPTIZED!"

Questions for Reflection

1. In what ways are baptisms celebrated with joy in your congregation?

2. Are those celebrations focused on the individual or family, or on the entire congregation? How?

Prayer

God of our life,
you spoke as Jesus was baptized, saying,
"This is my beloved Son . . ."
and you sent your Spirit to sustain him
throughout his time on earth.
We thank you and praise you
that you have called each of us by name,
sealing our adoption as your children
in baptism by water and your Spirit.
Guide us through every scene and season of our earthly life,
nurturing, equipping, and protecting,
until the day when we will see you face to face.
We ask this in Jesus' name. Amen.

Session 4-B: The Table of Plenty

A song from the United States

Come to the feast of heaven and earth!
Come to the table of plenty!
God will provide for all that we need,
here at the table of plenty.

My bread will ever sustain you
through days of sorrow and woe.
My wine will flow like a sea of gladness
to flood the depths of your soul.

4.3 Lord's Supper

Blessed is the church that regularly celebrates the Lord's Supper as a feast of thanksgiving, communion, and hope.

Blessed is the congregation that not only gratefully remembers God's creating and redeeming work in Jesus Christ, knowing his presence in the breaking of the bread, but also gratefully receives the gift of union with Jesus Christ and Christ's body, and looks forward to the feast of the coming kingdom.

Blessed is the congregation that shares this meal by "discerning the body of Christ" in its manifold oneness, by expressing hospitality for one another with grace and truth (1 Cor. 11:29-33), and by reflecting God's hospitality for us in ministries of hospitality in the world.

No other act of worship holds the central place of the Lord's Supper. Instituted by Jesus himself, the words and actions that take place around the table define us and our worship as "Christian."

This second sacrament instituted by Christ is known by many names, many of which are implied in these three proverbs:

- **Eucharist**, from the Greek *eucharistia*, means "thanksgiving." In 1 Corinthians 11:23-24, Paul says, "For I received from the Lord what I also passed on to you: The Lord Jesus, on the night he was betrayed, took bread, and when he had given thanks, he broke it and said, "This is my body, which is for you. Do this in remembrance of me."

- **"Lord's Supper"** is a term used in the early Church. It is taken from 1 Corinthians 11:20-21: "When you come together, it is not the Lord's Supper you eat, for when you are eating, some of you go ahead with your own private suppers. As a result, one person remains hungry and another gets drunk."

- **Communion** (or Holy Communion) comes from *communio*, the Latin translation of *koinonia,* which means "fellowship with God and with one another." It is found in 1 Corinthians 10:16 (NKJV): "The cup of blessing which we bless, is it not the communion of the blood of Christ? The bread which we break, is it not the communion of the body of Christ?"

No matter how often it is celebrated or what it is called, the Lord's Supper remains the greatest moment of our unity with Jesus Christ and with his disciples across continents and centuries. The different seasons of the Christian year offer many opportunities for variety in celebration. Let the Scriptures of the day determine the character of the celebration. Many churches always treat the service very somberly, akin to a funeral, remembering the death of Jesus. But celebrating the "Eucharist" on Christmas or on Easter should have an entirely different character.

James Torrance writes,

> [At] the Lord's Table, we do not merely remember the passion of our Lord as an isolated date from nineteen hundred years ago. Rather, we remember it in such a way that we know by the grace of God we are the people for whom our Savior died and rose again, we are the people whose sins Jesus confessed on the cross, we are the people with whom God has made a new covenant in the blood of Christ, we are the Israel of God to whom God has said, "I will be your God and you shall be my

people. . . ." We are what we are today by the grace of
God, because of what God did for us then.

—*Worship, Community & the Triune God of Grace*, InterVarsity, 1996, p. 84)

One way to visualize what is going on in this sacrament is to ask
whether it is primarily God's action (↓), or our response to what
God has done (↑), or perhaps primarily sharing a symbolic meal
with our fellow believers (↔). Some consider the Lord's Supper part of our response to the sermon. But Christ is the host! A
better way to consider the sacrament is in terms of the union we
have with Christ in this sacrament, in which we meet each other
in a distinct act, different from the conversation of alternating
proclamation and response that has taken place up to now in the
service. Perhaps the best way to "diagram" this covenant celebration is with an arrow that goes both ways; we are united with
Christ (↕). But there is more, because we should never consider
this a private moment between "me and Jesus," but as our communion also with each other (↔), united as the one body of
Christ (⟷). We are shaped by the cross to become cross-bearing
followers of Christ together.

The final proverb in this section returns the conversation to 1
Corinthians 11. Remember that Paul was addressing massive dys-
function within the congregation at Corinth. People of privilege
arrived early, ate and drank with no thought for others, became
drunk on the "blood of Christ" and gorged on his "body," and
not only disrupted the worship of the community but deprived
others of participation at the table. Middle Eastern translations
of this passage, more blunt than their English counterparts, help
us understand that Paul said these people were "destroying" the
body of Christ.

In his new commentary on 1 Corinthians, Kenneth Bailey captures the essence of the problem in Corinth and the truth behind
this proverb today:

> Paul's readers were asked to remember that [wor-
> ship] is not one more Greek drinking party. It is not
> merely a social occasion to pass the time with friends.
> . . . They have come together as the body of Christ to
> remember the saving events that created them as a
> body and to proclaim that salvation to the world. Each

worshiper is intimately connected with the other worshipers, and the struggles, joys, fears, and failures of all are known and shared. All come as sinners in need of grace, and in that shared awareness there is openness to receive needed healing. The only believer who is unworthy to receive the Holy Communion is the person who thinks that he/she is worthy to receive it.

—from *Paul Through Mediterranean Eyes*, InterVarsity Press, 2011, pp. 323-324

Before we leave this study of baptism and the Lord's Supper, consider their deep connection.

Baptism is an initiation into the covenant community, dying and rising with Christ to new life (Rom. 6:3-4). Baptism happens once, but we need continuing nourishment. The historic pattern of Christian worship is to include both Word and table. In fact, all good preaching leads to the table, because there we have the opportunity to celebrate our fellowship with our risen Lord and to be nourished by him to live out the call God has placed on our lives and to which we make promises again each week in our prayers and offerings. Both Word and table provide nourishment for our faith.

In the last fifty years, many churches around the world have increased the frequency of celebrating the Lord's Supper. This practice helps to restore a balance that was lost in the sixteenth century, when Roman Catholics neglected the Word in favor of the table, and in reaction many Protestants broke the ancient connection between Word and table, and ended up neglecting the table in favor of the Word.

Here are five practices that may help your congregation deepen their understanding of the relationship between baptism and the Lord's Supper:

1. Set the font in full view of the worshipping community.

2. Open the font and fill it with water every Lord's Day.

3. Set cup and plate on the Lord's table every Lord's Day.

4. Lead portions of weekly worship from the font and table, for example,

a. at the font, leading the prayer of confession and declaration of pardon, expressing our confidence in God's forgiveness in our baptismal identity; lifting water with hand as words of forgiveness are spoken).

b. at the table, leading the prayers of intercession; the table is where the hungry are fed. Our prayers come into focus as we reach out to the world.

5. Increase the number of Sundays on which the Lord's Supper is celebrated.

—from *Invitation to Christ—Extended*, Association for Reformed and Liturgical Worship, 2012

Questions for Reflection

1. Does your celebration of the Lord's Supper differ in different seasons of the year? If so, how?

2. What truths does the sacrament of the Lord's Supper tell us about ourselves, our worshiping community, and our place in God's big picture?

3. Part of the celebration of the Lord's Supper is the "great prayer of thanksgiving." Locate several versions of this prayer in *The Worship Sourcebook* (Faith Alive/Baker/CICW), the *Book of Common Worship* (PCUSA), and in other worship books, and discuss ways in which content is the same and different in each of them.

4. What part of this study was new to you, or most helpful?

Prayer

Great and loving God, Father, Son, and Spirit,
when we come to your table
we remember Jesus' perfect sacrifice of love,
and we give our endless thanks for our salvation in him.
When we go from your table,
keep us in communion with you and with each other:
a sign of your promised kingdom and reign.
Christ has died!
Christ is risen!
Christ will come again!
Alleluia! Amen.

⬆ *Circle of Light,* by Paul Stoub, United States. Used by permission.

Session 5: Blessed and Commissioned

Go, my children, with my blessing, never alone.
Waking, sleeping, I am with you; you are my own.
In my love's baptismal river
I have made you mine forever.
Go, my children, with my blessing; you are my own.

Go, my children, sins forgiven, at peace and pure.
Here you learned how much I love you, what I can cure.
Here you heard my dear Son's story;
here you touched him, saw his glory.
Go, my children, sins forgiven, at peace and pure.

Go, my children, fed and nourished, closer to me.
Grow in love and love by serving, joyful and free.
Here my Spirit's power filled you;
here his tender comfort stilled you.
Go, my children, fed and nourished, joyful and free.

I, the Lord, will bless and keep you, and give you peace.
I, the Lord, will smile upon you, and give you peace.
I, the Lord, will be your Father,
Savior, Comforter, and Brother.
Go, my children. I will keep you, and give you peace.

What does it mean to be "a blessed and commissioned people serving in Jesus' name" (WTG section 5)? The answer to that question defines our expectations of worship.

Disciples of Jesus gather for worship seeking a deeper fellowship with God and our fellow believers. Jesus Christ is God's ultimate blessing. In *The Message*, Eugene Peterson contextualized John 1:14 with these words: "The Word became flesh and blood and moved into the neighborhood. We saw the glory with our own eyes, the one-of-a-kind glory, like Father, like Son, generous inside and out, true from start to finish." In Jesus Christ, God has come to us, reconciling us to himself and entrusting us with the message of reconciliation (2 Cor. 5:19). The final act of our communal worship is where that good news gets its feet, when we receive God's blessing and call to discipleship.

God's blessing is not the end of the story, however. Jesus' commission to his disciples leaves no room for doubt that we are blessed to be a blessing. Again from *The Message*: "Go out and train everyone you meet, far and near, in this way of life, marking them by baptism in the threefold name: Father, Son, and Holy Spirit. Then instruct them in the practice of all I have commanded. I'll be with you as you do this, day after day after day, right up to the end of the age" (Matt. 28:19-20).

The primary purpose of the church and its worship is not to attract, drawing people in, but to equip and send God's redeemed people into mission in the world.

This understanding of the core mission of the church impacts our expectations for worship. If God's primary desire was for a church with full seats and never-ending activities, we would focus time, effort, and resources on making our congregation more attractive and appealing than any of the neighboring churches. But Scripture reveals that God's singular desire is the redemption of the world, and that Christ has commissioned the Church to continue his work on earth in the power of the Holy Spirit. To the extent that we realize this, our time, efforts, and resources will be focused on nurturing disciples of Jesus who expect to actively participate in God's mission and who will fully engage in the life of the worshiping community to prepare for that sending.

Session 5-A: Where Liturgy Stops and Life Begins

A song from South Africa

Thuma mina,	Send me, Jesus,
thuma mina,	send me, Jesus,
thuma mina,	send me, Jesus,
somandla.	send me, Lord.

From: "Thuma mina/Send Me, Lord"
Words: South African © 1984 Peasce of Music AB, admin. Walton Music Corporation

A song from Argentina

¡Dios de la esperanza, danos gozo y paz!
Al mundo en crisis, habla tu verdad.
Dios de la justicia, mándanos tu luz.
Luz y esperanza en la oscuridad.

May the God of hope go with us every day,
filling all our lives with love and joy and peace.
May the God of justice speed us on our way,
bringing light and hope to every land and race.

From: "Canto de esperanza/Song of Hope"
Words: st. 1 Spanish traditional; English tr. Alvin Schutmaat (1921-1988)

5.1 God's Sending

Blessed is the congregation in which believers are encouraged by God's gracious blessing and challenged by God's gracious call to proclaim the good news of Jesus and to live as a healing presence in the world in the name of Jesus.

The first proverb in this final section has two parts: God's blessing and God's call. We are blessed to be a blessing, echoing God's plan throughout the history of the covenant, first spoken by God to Abraham (Gen. 12:1-3).

⊙ The chapel of Trinity College in Singapore is above the library, making the point that the worship of God is above the pursuit of knowledge. The roof is in the shape of the Chinese character for humanity (ren-人), symbolizing that the worship of God is the primary purpose of humanity."

Just as God greets us at the beginning of our communal worship with words of welcome and peace, so we leave with God's words of blessing or "benediction," which means "to speak a good word." The historic blessing found in Numbers 6:24-26 was not Moses' word to the people of Israel; the words were given directly by God to Moses. There are many other blessings in Scripture that are also appropriate; the words may be connected to the theme of the service, but always must be received as a gift: the "good word" from God that empowers disciples for service.

The parting blessing is not the pastor's "good word" of encouragement to the congregation (⟷); it's a proclamation (↓). God speaks once more his covenant promise to be with us, so that when we leave we do not go in our own strength, but in the power and with the blessing of God. The tradition of an ordained pastor raising both hands in blessing is almost universal, as though placing hands on the heads of everyone there. Even in churches that practice little physical movement, an old tradition is for the congregation to receive the blessing with bowed heads and closed eyes. Some churches have encouraged a newer practice so as to become more conscious of receiving this blessing: extending open hands, palms up, and perhaps receiving the blessing with eyes wide open.

Now we are able to act on the second part, God's call. Here again, the words of this charge, or call to discipleship, may come directly from Scripture, because indeed, God is the One calling us. The content of that call may reflect the particular message in the sermon of that day, but always will include the challenge to discipleship.

There is one more time-honored practice among Christians for the concluding part of our communal worship: a "doxology," or a song of praise to God who has so loved and blessed us. God calls and blesses, and our joyful response is to receive this call with praise and dedication. The order of these three parts—praise, commissioning, and blessing—may differ, but all three are a fitting conclusion to our communal worship.

After the congregation has assembled for worship in Jesus' name, joyfully proclaimed God's Word, responded with prayer and offerings, celebrated our faith at the font and at the table, and received God's blessing and call, we are sent ". . . into the neighborhood" so others can see with their own eyes the "one-of-a-kind glory" of Jesus revealed in us; like Savior, like people, ". . . generous and just inside and out, true from start to finish."

When disciples of Jesus are sent into the world, our commission is to become, "salt and light" (Matt. 5:13-16), people who, as Stanley Hauerwas writes, "are faithful to their promises, love their enemies, tell the truth, honor the poor, suffer for righteousness, and thereby testify to the amazing community-creating power of God . . . a living, breathing, visible community of faith" (*Resident Aliens*, Abingdon Press, 1989, p. 293). And yet, this act of intentional sending is often neglected or minimized in the structure of our worship.

A worshiping community without a proper sending is like a restaurant without a functioning wait staff trained to use their expertise, imagination, and passion to feed hungry people. God prepares us through worship and sets us apart to use our knowledge of Scripture, God's plan and purpose, and our personal and communal experience of God's grace to transform daily life in a fallen world. Our great honor as the people God has called is to participate in the drama of redemption that includes every person and every part of God's creation.

Questions for Reflection

1. In what ways does the parting blessing encourage you? Do you receive this as applying directly to you for the coming week?

2. Similarly, in what ways does the charge, or the call to service, challenge and commission you for the coming week?

A song from Tanzania

Guide our thinking and our speaking
done in your holy name.
Motivate all in their seeking,
freeing from guilt and pain.

Keep us fervent in our witness,
unswayed by earth's allure.
Ever grant us zealous fitness,
which you alone ensure.

Come, come, come, Holy Spirit, come.
Njoo, njoo, njoo, Roho mwema.

From: "Gracious Spirit, Heed Our Pleading"
Words: Wilson Niwaglia, 20th c. Tanzania; tr. Howard S. Olson (b. 1922); arr. C. Michael Hawn (b. 1948) © Lutheran Theological College, Makumira, Tanzania, admin. Augsburg Fortress Publishers

5.2 Daily Worship

Wise is the community that nourishes faith by encouraging daily worship for all believers, with emphasis on reading and meditating on God's Word, seeking the guidance of the Holy Spirit, offering prayers of praise and petition, singing psalms, hymns, and spiritual songs, listening for God in "sheer silence" (1 Kings 19:12), and living every moment before the face of God.

◉ Praying the psalms in Pakistan

The origins of daily worship can be traced to the Jerusalem temple. Every morning and every evening, sacrifices were made, accompanied by prayers and psalms. In the book of Deuteronomy, the Law of God is followed by the *shema*: "Hear, O Israel, the LORD our God, the LORD is one. Love the LORD your God with all your heart and with all your soul and with all your strength" (Deut. 6:4-5). The text continues, "These commandments that I give you today are to be on your hearts. Impress them on your children. Talk about them when you sit at home and when you walk along the road, when you lie down and when you get up. Tie them as symbols on your hands and bind them on your foreheads. Write them on the doorframes of your houses and on your gates" (Deut. 6:6-9).

Hughes Oliphant Old writes, "For classical Reformed spirituality, morning and evening family prayer was one of the foundations of piety. It was at the heart of the day-to-day exercising of Christian faith. This made sense to those for whom Covenant theology was informative. The unity of the family was a significant feature of Covenant theology. With the coming of Pietism, daily family prayer was unfortunately replaced with private devotions" (*Scripture Reformed According to Scripture*, John Knox Press, 1984, p. 148).

TESTIMONY

Each morning about 6:30 and evening about 7:00, the family we were staying with—an older couple with six children they had taken in—gathered and began to clap their hands. Someone would start to sing, and they went from one song to the next. Then one of the parents would ask, "Who would like to preach tonight?" and one of the children would read a passage of Scripture they had selected and offer comment on its meaning. For our sake, they spoke in English (an official language of Nigeria, and taught in the schools) rather than in Tiv, their mother tongue. Then the mother would ask, "Does anyone have anything to add [to the interpretation]"? Perhaps someone would add something, and one of the parents would also provide some interpretation. Then the parents asked, "Who would like to pray?" And two or three would offer to pray, which they did in Tiv, pouring out their hearts to God. We ended by saying the Lord's Prayer together. What training in Scripture and prayer! These children were ready and willing to participate in front of guests, who were during this week simply part of the family circle.

—Emily Brink, diary from a visit to Mkar, Nigeria

While a schedule of daily prayer (morning, midday, evening, and night are the traditional times) provides abundant, meaningful opportunities for deepening our life of faith, many contemporary people will need to begin more modestly. Consciously "living every moment before the face of God" can start with a simple act of commitment to memorizing and repeating verses of Scripture or a hymn, remembering people we encounter and their various needs in our prayers, or allocating time for "sheer silence" and listening to God. For parents, modeling daily prayer and Scripture reading together as a family is of great value, perhaps at some agreed-upon (meal?) times during the week where you can manage to be together—an increasingly difficult challenge in overly busy societies. Here are some other suggestions:

- Set aside time with members of your family, or others you see regularly, to pray, read Scripture, and sing a hymn or psalm.

- Read a passage of Scripture in the morning and the same passage at night. Prayerfully consider how your experiences through the day changed the way you hear or understand that portion of God's Word.

- Dedicate time to reading Scripture slowly, allowing yourself to be distracted by a particular word or phrase and allowing the Holy Spirit time to speak to you in that "distraction." Then keep that Scripture in your mind as you move through your day. What is God showing you?

- Sing hymns and worship songs attentively when you worship with your congregation. What thoughts or images catch your imagination and stay with you into the week?

- Memorize words and melodies of the psalms, hymns, and spiritual songs you sing in corporate worship. Allow the Holy Spirit to speak to you throughout the week.

- At the beginning of each day, consciously pray for the people you expect to meet. During the day, pray for the needs, hopes, hurts, and desires you hear people express.

- Pray the news—what you read and what you hear on the media.

- Use your "down time" between projects, meetings, or conversations to pray for the people and situations you are encountering and the joys or frustrations of the day, or to listen for God in silence.

- Build times of intentional silence into your day: turn off the iPod and the TV, move away from the computer, close the door, be still.

- Then, at the end of the day, testify to someone—companion, friend, spouse, children—how you sensed God's leading and how God answered your prayers. This act of testimony is one simple way of practicing our faith in an open way before others so that our words as well as our deeds give glory to God and encouragement to others—and to ourselves.

In every conversation, every situation, every decision, and every action, we have the opportunity to move closer to God and be a witness to his redeeming love, or further away from God and the life for which we have been commissioned. Daily worship helps us make wise choices, giving us not only the tools for deepening our faith, but practice in applying Scripture and prayer to daily living so that, when truly challenging seasons come along, we are prepared to meet them with the power of God's Word and the certainty of God's presence (see Matt. 4:1-11).

Questions for Reflection

1. How can worshiping communities encourage their people to develop a deeper life of daily worship?

2. What elements from the communal worship of your community can easily be transferred into daily worship?

3. How can you help your people prepare each week for the Scripture, music, and focus of corporate worship?

Let us build a house where hands will reach
beyond the wood and stone
to heal and strengthen, serve and teach,
and live the Word they've known.
Here the outcast and the stranger
bear the image of God's face;
let us bring an end to fear and danger:
All are welcome, all are welcome,
all are welcome in this place.

5.3   Hospitality and Evangelization

Blessed are communities in which hospitality is practiced in both public worship and in personal lives, where strangers and guests are welcomed and embraced, where the poor and marginalized, diseased and forsaken can find refuge under the shadow of God's wings.

Blessed are communities in which all people are invited and challenged to become disciples of Jesus, receiving baptism and formation in the faith (cf Matt. 28:19).

❸ Sunday school children in the state of Mizoram, India

❸ Sunday afternoon recorder class before playing a hymn in the evening service in Aguilares, El Salvador

112

Tod Bolsinger writes, "The transforming community of the church is meant to be the place where we genuinely experience and sincerely extend the love of the Trinity. By our lives and with our lips, we witness to that which we have experienced and invite others to partake; we bear witness to how our lives have been transformed and offer that same life-transforming power to others" (*It Takes a Church to Raise a Christian*, Brazos Press, 2004, p. 141).

The song text by Marty Haugen quoted above provides words of welcome for the opening of a worship service; so does Joseph Hart's 1759 hymn "Come, Ye Sinners": "Come, ye sinners, poor and needy, weak and wounded, sick and sore; Jesus ready stands to save you, full of mercy, love, and power." Those words were written by an antagonist toward Christianity whose subsequent experience of God's transforming grace and the patient nurture of Christian peers led him to become one of the most influential preachers of his day in the city of London. Both songs speak the gospel: Jesus Christ is willing to meet us wherever we are, and because Christ is Redeemer, he is not willing to leave us there.

As Christ's disciples in the world, we are called to embody the same combination of compassion and commitment, law and gospel, truth and grace. This is very good news, but proclaiming it is seriously countercultural. Jesus offended the religious leaders of his day by eating and drinking with sinners. Jesus was willing to associate with anyone, not in judgment, but in compassion; in fact, his greatest words of frustration were for the religious leaders who wanted people to measure up to their laws and regulations before considering them worthy of their attention.

Our call is to build communities of welcome, regardless of our differences. This is a significant challenge for people who don't often associate with others not like themselves. Learning to offer welcome in worship is not unlike showing hospitality in our homes. Visiting other worshiping communities can be instructive—and revealing! How were you welcomed? Were you encouraged to participate? Were you encouraged and enabled to participate even in the elements of worship that were unfamiliar to you? The welcome that disciples of Jesus extend must be genuine and must carry through all ministries of the church as we connect in meaningful ways with our neighborhoods and the broader community. In this way our worship will both shape and be consistent with our witness.

The Presbyterian Church (USA)'s 1967 *Book of Confessions* states, "The church disperses to serve God wherever its members are, at work or play, in private or in the life of society. Their prayer and Bible study are part of the church's worship and theological reflection. Their witness is the church's evangelism. Their daily action in the world is the church in mission to the world. The quality of their relation with other persons is the measure of the church's fidelity" (9.37).

Questions for Reflection

1. How does concern for hospitality and evangelism shape and influence your congregation's worship?

2. Who are the "poor and needy, sick and sore" in your neighborhood?

3. A different question: who are the "lepers" and "outcasts" in our society?

4. How could they all receive a welcome in your worshiping community? Are their lives different because worshipers of the triune God live and worship near them?

Prayer

> Unwavering and faithful triune God,
> you greet us each morning
> with joy and mercy sufficient for the day.
> You watch over us each night,
> overcoming our fears and anxieties with your peace.
> Give us a hunger to remain in your presence,
> and overwhelm us with your love.
> We can ask this only because of Jesus. Amen.

Session 5-B: Preparing for God's Future—and Ours

A song from the United States

Match the present to the promise,
Christ will come again.
Make this hope your guiding premise,
Christ will come again.
Pattern all your calculating
and the world you are creating
to the advent you are waiting:
Christ will come again.

From: "View the Present Through the Promise"
Words: Thomas H. Troeger, (b. 1945) © Oxford University Press Inc., 1986, assigned to Oxford University Press 2010, reproduced by permission

5.4 Formation for Worship

Wise are congregations that invite and challenge believers of all ages and abilities to "grow in the grace and knowledge of our Lord and Savior Jesus Christ" (2 Pet. 3:18).

Blessed are congregations that nurture the faithful interplay of Scripture, doctrines, practices, and the fruit of the Spirit.

Wise are congregations that deepen worship through reflection on and teaching about the meaning of worship practices.

At every stage of life, parents and civic leaders attempt to teach vital life practices, especially when it comes to safety and health. In the church, Sunday school and education programs help children and adults learn about the content of our faith and how to apply it in our lives. We learn best as children by modeling what our parents do. Children and new believers grow in their understanding of worship by becoming imitators of those more mature in the faith.

As we have seen throughout this conversation about worship, everyone—regardless of age, culture, or condition—is capable of learning how to sing and how to pray (and discovering why God's

115

◐ At the Assyrian Presbyterian Church in Baghdad, the children lead an Advent service with "We Three Kings of Orient Are," not far from the very place from which the Magi might have begun their journey.

◑ Worship in Hong Kong

◐ Sunday school children singing in Aizawl, Mizoram, India

◑ Girls' choir in Mkar, Nigeria

◑ Children's choir in
Singapore

◐ Hong Kong youth at a
worship conference

⬆ Teaching youth worship songs in
Jaguey Grande, Cuba

⬆ Children at
worship in Pakistan

◑ Father on keyboard
and son on accordion
helping to lead
worship in El Salvador

people must do both!), what it means to confess sin, and why we can be assured of God's unconditional love. Each worshiping congregation wisely connects people with the triune God through images, practices, music, movement, and media that speak most clearly to that particular group of people, drawing a conglomeration of individuals into a community of worshipers, and then dispersing those who have encountered the triune God back into the world as contagious ambassadors of all they have seen, heard, and experienced.

Questions for Reflection

1. How and when do you "teach" people to worship in your congregation?

2. How could a child, visitor, or someone new to the faith be nurtured in the practices of worship by imitating you?

3. In what ways does the "fruit of the Spirit" (Gal. 5:22, 23) that we continue to develop in our own lives influence the nurturing of our fellow worshipers?

A song from Spain

Oremos por la paz,	Praying, let us work for peace,
cantemos de tu amor,	singing, share our joy with all,
luchemos por la paz,	working for a world that's new,
fieles a ti Señor.	faithful when we hear Christ's call.

From: "Canto de esperanza/Song of Hope"
Words: st. 2 Tom Mitchell (b. 1947) © 1993 Choristers Guild; Sp. Tr. Frank W. Roman (b. 20th c.)

5.5 Worship, Compassion, and Justice

Blessed are congregations whose public worship points to Jesus Christ and to Jesus' message about the kingdom of God.

Blessed are congregations whose corporate worship and public witness are consistent with each other and faithful to God's Word, whose worship and witness are a testimony to the work of the Holy Spirit.

Blessed are congregations who seek to receive the liberating work of the Holy Spirit, who alone can break through hypocrisy and through whom justice and peace, worship and witness, can truly embrace.

Our prayers of intercession and the focus of our offerings are the place where our worship brings the needs of the world most clearly before God and before our own hearts, so that we may discern God's call on us to respond. But those needs are gathered up also in the closing words of a call to service. Prayerfully read and discuss the words of the following charge and benediction. It captures the essence and the challenge of these three proverbs as God's people—forgiven, loved, and freed—are deployed in mission:

> Because the world is poor and starving, go with bread.
> Because the world is filled with fear, go with courage.
> Because the world is in despair, go with hope.
> Because the world is living lies, go with truth.
> Because the world is sick with sorrow, go with joy.
> Because the world is weary of wars, go with peace.
> Because the world is seldom fair, go with justice.
> Because the world is under judgment, go with mercy.
> Because the world will die without it, go with love.
> It is God who will give you the grace and strength to do all these things.
> Go in the grace of Christ Jesus, and may all glory go to Him! Amen.
>
> —written in 1995 by Hal Warheim, adapted by Rebecca Heid. Used by permission.

Questions for Reflection

1. In what ways does the worship of your congregation most clearly point to Jesus Christ and to God's kingdom?

2. In what ways has your congregation sought justice and peace as expressions of the kingdom of God?

3. What evidence have you seen of the Holy Spirit breaking through hypocrisy and uniting justice and worship in a common witness?

5.6   Maranatha: Worship and Christian Hope

Blessed are congregations who are not content to live only in the present moment, but whose worship expresses the groaning of all creation for the fullness of God's reign in Jesus Christ.

Blessed are congregations whose life together is summed up in the certain hope of the prayer "Maranatha—come, Lord Jesus" (Rev. 22:20).

These final proverbs, like the charge and benediction at the close of worship, take us still further beyond ourselves. Our experience of God's blessing multiplies exponentially when we eagerly anticipate and actively seek interaction with God—Father, Son, and Holy Spirit. As we move from the joy of worshiping together, blessed by God with glimpses of the way the world is supposed to be, we enter our groaning world that longs for redemption (Rom. 8:22).

But even more than this, our communal worship reminds us that the life we now experience is itself a nanosecond of the reality of God's eternity, and that the Creator of the cosmos invites us beyond ourselves into his limitless hope and joy. The world we now see, fallen and flawed, will one day be redeemed and restored to its original beauty and God's original intent.

We close this section and this conversation with the final stanza of "It Is Well with My Soul," a nineteenth-century hymn that is experiencing renewed popularity in many worshiping communities, including among young adults. May these enduring words of hope and promise live on your lips and in your heart as you worship the triune God and invite others to do the same. Then, as disciples of Jesus who have worshiped the triune God, follow God into mission—wherever that mission may lead us in God's world.

And Lord, haste the day when my faith shall be sight,
the clouds be rolled back as a scroll;
the trumpet shall sound, and the Lord shall descend.
Even so, it is well with my soul!

From: "When Peace Like a River"
Words: Horatio G. Spafford, 1873, P.D.

Questions for Reflection

1. Where/how do you most clearly hear the creation "groaning" for the fullness of God's reign?

2. How is/can that groaning be expressed through worship of the triune God?

3. When we pray, "Come, Lord Jesus!" what images, hopes, and expectations come to your mind?

4. How has this study and your discussions challenged you in how you worship and in your mission and service to others?

Now to him who by the power at work within us
is able to accomplish abundantly far more
than all we can ask or imagine,
to him be glory in the church
and in Christ Jesus to all generations,
for ever and ever. Amen. (Eph. 3:20-22, NRSV)

Prayer

God of all time and space, Father, Son, and Holy Spirit,
wherever we go, you have sent us;
show us your plan and purpose.
Whatever we experience, you are with us;
strengthen us in your grace, love, and power,
Make us your faithful disciples until you return.
Maranatha! Come, Lord Jesus!

Appendix 1: Components of Christian Worship

Now the Silence

GATHER:	Now the silence, now the peace, now the empty hands uplifted.
CONFESS:	Now the kneeling, now the plea,
ASSURANCE:	now the Father's arms in welcome.
PROCLAIM:	Now the hearing, now the power,
GIVE AN OFFERING:	now the vessel brimmed for pouring.
CELEBRATE:	Now the Body, now the Blood, now the joyful celebration.
UNITE WITH CHRIST:	Now the wedding, now the songs, now the heart forgiven leaping.
GO IN GOD'S NAME:	Now the Spirit's visitation, now the Son's epiphany, now the Father's blessing, now, now, now.

Across continents and centuries, irrespective of local dialects or customs, Christian worship is distinctive in its form and content. Different congregations, denominations, or movements may vary the order of worship, but, with few exceptions, all of these component parts have deep biblical precedent and will be included. Far more than traditionalism, this is Christian tradition, uniting twenty-first-century worshipers with disciples throughout the past two millennia.

Worship on the Lord's Day

From its beginnings, the Christian community has gathered on the first day of the week to hear the Scriptures read and proclaimed and to celebrate the Lord's Supper. The first day has special significance since it marks the day Christ rose from the grave.

For early Christians, the resurrection of Jesus Christ was an event to remember and celebrate. The resurrection authenticated Jesus' ministry, defeated the power of death, and gave assurance of eternal life. Recognizing the importance of the resurrection, the New Testament community called that day of the week on which Christ rose "the Lord's Day." It was the day to celebrate.

The Lord's Day, the first day of the week, is the very pivot point of the church's calendar. In the ancient story of creation, this day marked the beginning of creation. God spoke light into being, separating light from darkness. In Christ's resurrection, Christians saw the beginning of the "new creation" and came to regard the day of resurrection as "the eighth day of creation." The Lord's Day is a sign of God's kingdom and of hope. "On the Lord's Day I was in the Spirit, and I heard behind me a loud voice like a trumpet . . ." (Rev. 1:10)

Gather

Worship begins with God. God takes the initiative and calls us into being. In the name of Christ we heed God's call and assemble as the community of faith.

> Therefore, brothers and sisters, since we have confidence to enter the Most Holy Place by the blood of Jesus, by a new and living way opened for us through the curtain, that is, his body, and since we have a great priest over the house of God, let us draw near to God with a sincere heart and with the full assurance that faith brings. . . . Let us hold unswervingly to the hope we profess, for he who promised is faithful. And let us consider how we may spur one another on toward love and good deeds, not giving up meeting together, as some are in the habit of doing, but encouraging one another—and all the more as you see the Day approaching (Heb. 10:19-25).

Praise

Praise and adoration are the keynotes of all true worship, of the creature before the Creator, of the redeemed before the Redeemer. In song and prayer, God is praised.

> Sing to the LORD a new song;
> sing to the LORD, all the earth.
> Sing to the LORD, praise his name;
> proclaim his salvation day after day.
> Declare his glory among the nations,
> his marvelous deeds among all peoples.
> For great is the LORD and most worthy of praise;
> he is to be feared above all gods.
> For all the gods of the nations are idols,
> but the LORD made the heavens.
> Splendor and majesty are before him;
> strength and glory are in his sanctuary (Psalm 96:1-6).

Confess Our Sin

Before God's majesty and holiness, we become painfully aware of our selfishness and disobedience. We repent of our sin and ask God's forgiveness. We cannot earn God's forgiveness by our repentance, nor can we ever be worthy of God's mercy. It is only in the assurance of God's prior mercy given freely to the undeserving that we dare make our humble confession before God.

> "If we claim to be without sin, we deceive ourselves and the truth is not in us. If we confess our sins, [God] is faithful and just and will forgive us our sins and purify us from all unrighteousness" (1 John 1:8, 9).

Proclaim God's Word

We first pray that the Holy Spirit may illumine our hearts and minds so that we may hear and be prepared to accept God's Word for us. Readings from both the Old and New Testaments ensure that the unity and completeness of God's revelation are proclaimed.

The God who speaks in Scripture also speaks to us now. The God who acted in biblical history acts today. Rooted in Scripture, faithful preaching confronts us with the liberating Word and witnesses to God's continuing activity among us and in the life of the world.

"Your word is a lamp for my feet and a light on my path" (Ps. 119:105).

"'Everyone who calls on the name of the Lord will be saved.' How, then, can they call on the one they have not believed in? And how can they believe in the one of whom they have not heard? And how can they hear without someone preaching to them? And how can anyone preach unless they are sent?" (Rom. 10:13-15a)

Pray

Across the ages, the church in its worship has prayed for the church universal, the world, all in authority, and those in distress or need. At no other time in its worship is the community of faith more conscious of the needs of the life of the world. We pray for the world because God loves the world. God created it and cares for it. God sent Jesus, who died for it. God is working to lead it toward the future God has for it. To abide in God's love is to share God's concern for the world. Our prayers should be as wide as God's love and as specific as God's compassion for the least ones among us. "If you abide in me, and my words abide in you, ask for whatever you wish, and it will be done for you. My Father is glorified by this, that you bear much fruit and become my disciples" (John 15:7-8, NRSV).

Give an Offering

Having prayed for the world, we put ourselves where our prayers are. In grateful response to the abundance of God's grace, we offer ourselves to be instruments of God's peace, love, and justice. As stewards, we give from what God has given us, acknowledging that the world is not ours but God's. "For where your treasure is, there your heart will be also" (Luke 12:34).

Celebrate Baptism

Baptism is both a personal and a communal experience. Persons to be baptized are surrounded at the font by members of the worshiping congregation. Promises of faith and faithfulness are made by everyone. God's saving acts are remembered with thanksgiving, along with the realization that God loved us first, and nothing can separate us from that love. Baptism marks a life-changing event. It is a profound initiation into a new community.

As the apostle Paul writes,

> Or don't you know that all of us who were baptized into Christ Jesus were baptized into his death? We were therefore buried with him through baptism into death in order that, just as Christ was raised from the dead through the glory of the Father, we too may live a new life. For if we have been united with him in a death like his, we will certainly also be united with him in a resurrection like his. For we know that our old self was crucified with him so that the body ruled by sin might be done away with, that we should no longer be slaves to sin—because anyone who has died has been set free from sin (Rom. 6:3-7).

Celebrate the Lord's Supper

Like baptism, communion is both a personal and a communal experience. The sacrament is for each person, but we gather at the Lord's table not simply as individuals. We come to the table as members together of God's family, the body of Christ, the church. The Lord's Supper is the family meal of the people of God. "For whenever you eat this bread and drink this cup, you proclaim the Lord's death until he comes" (1 Cor. 11:26).

Go in God's Name

> We praise God for Christ's presence with us in Word and Sacrament, and we claim the strength and guidance of the Holy Spirit as we move out into ministry.

> We are commissioned to obedient and grateful ministry as God's agents to heal life's brokenness. By the power of the Spirit let us be what Christ has redeemed us to be.

> The blessing of the triune God is given. Assured of God's peace and blessing, we are confident that God goes with us to our tasks.

> "Therefore go and make disciples of all nations, baptizing them in the name of the Father and of the Son and of the Holy Spirit, and teaching them to obey everything I have commanded you. And surely I am with you always, to the very end of the age" (Matt. 28:19-20).

—Harold Daniels, SLR:1 Service for the Lord's Day, 1984, with Scripture verses added by Paul Detterman

Appendix 2 : The Worship Planner's List of Virtues

- compassion for the congregation's needs and concern about how those needs are addressed in worship;

- discernment about who is gifted to lead worship and in what way;

- cooperativeness for working on a team of people involved in planning and leading worship;

- knowledge of God's Word and of which portions of it are especially important for a congregation to hear at a given time, as well as knowledge of the community and its particular pastoral needs;

- wisdom to understand the psychological and theological issues involved when there is conflict about worship;

- patience when the congregation is slow to participate fully in certain acts of worship;

- imagination to generate ideas about which songs, scripts, prayers, and elements will engage a congregation with the power and meaning of a given scriptural theme;

- discipline to avoid too much or too little innovation. Planning worship is far different from putting on an art fair or writing poetry. When we plan worship, we are planning something for a community's use. No community can sustain endless innovation. No community can truly pray with words that are entirely unfamiliar or are creative for their own sake. Nor can a community thrive if its worship never changes in response to its environment.

These are the kinds of traits that go beyond the mechanics of worship planning to worship's deeper purpose and meaning. Perhaps this list makes you feel inadequate, but remember that none of us has all these virtues naturally. And no one can live up to all these virtues all of the time. But the good news of New Testament living is that these traits are not only ideals that we strive for; they are also gifts that the Holy Spirit gives to a community of believers for building up the church. The first step in worship planning is to pray that the Spirit will nurture these kinds of virtues in you. And for whichever virtues you lack, look to others in your congregation who may share them. Worship planning happens best in collaboration! Good resources also play a small but important role. While effective priestly prayer-leadership can arise only out of a life of prayer, even the most effective prayer life cannot prepare us to lead a whole congregation in prayer. We need to learn from others, from worship in other places and times, and—mostly—from Scripture.

—*The Worship Sourcebook*, Faith Alive Christian Resources/Baker/CICW, 2004, pp. 19-20